LITERARY GASTRONOMY

D0840823

Rodopi Perspectives on Modern Literature

1

Edited by

David Bevan

LITERARY GASTRONOMY

Edited by
David Bevan

AMSTERDAM 1988

©Editions Rodopi B.V., Amsterdam 1988
ISBN 90—5183—062—9 (CIP)
Printed in The Netherlands

CONTENTS

Dis-moi ce que tu manges,
je te dirai ce que tu es ...

(Brillat-Savarin, 1825)

INTRODUCTION

> ... la voration: engloutissement
> primitif d'un être par un autre, puis
> sa digestion, son assimilation. (...)
> l'interpénétration, prenant alors
> valeur cosmique, devient une des
> catégories de l'appétit: "Toute la
> nature que nous avons sous les
> yeux est mangeante et mangée.
> Les proies s'entremordent."
>
> (J.-P. Richard)[1]

After *homo sapiens*, *homo ludens*, *homo necans et al*, the present volume seeks to record the pervasiveness and the significance in this century of *homo edens*. For what Brillat-Savarin projected over one hundred and fifty years ago has acquired a resonance and a centrality today that is admirably and exhaustively inscribed in text.

Already, an excellent recent special number of *Dalhousie French Studies*, "Littérature et Nourriture", has examined in this regard that literary production which is the immediate pre-history to our own times. In his introduction to that collection, James Brown usefully posits a relationship, both metaphoric and essential, between food and literature, which sees them as twin "transformational and generative processes. In both instances, the world is endlessly assimilated, transformed and remade. Phagos/Logos."[2] Certainly, in terms of twentieth century fiction, this relationship has occasioned latterly, not only a fulsome spate of studies that shows no sign of dwindling, but also regular oral (!) activity at the influential annual gatherings of the Modern Languages' Association of America, and even the approaching "consecration" that is ultimately signalled in such fermentation by an impulse towards categorisation, a classificatory system ... Michel Rybalka's Gallic ruminations of Fourier's *gastrosophie* into *gastrotexte* and *cénasthésie* being, perhaps, most worthy of retention to date.

But, despite occasional nationalistic claims to the contrary, neither culinary artistry nor gastro-alimentary discourse are

limited to France. Recognition of the filiation ingestion/expression
in all its avatars is obviously far more extensive, and never more so
than at a time and in a world increasingly contaminated by the
residual effects of synthetic products and toxic sprays; in a variety
of forms the very deep throat of noxious commercialism has added
to the general truth of Brillat-Savarin's observation a rumble that
is glaringly apocalyptic.

In the essays which follow, the phenomenon of literary
gastronomy is registered and monitored across several continents,
widely differing cultural traditions and assorted individual
predilections. Nor are the critical perspectives any less rich, for, if
the semiological is served universally, the garnishes - Freudian,
feminist, Jungian, structuralist etc. - are appropriately various.
Moreover, the multiple manifestations and operations of the
digestive tract constitute, properly, a *corpus* that can inform and
signal a preoccupation with sundry bodies - politic, psycho-sexual,
social, anthropological and, above all, ontological. South Africa,
Fascism, eroticism, emancipation, materialism, cannibalism are
amongst the points of reference in a Malrucian-style colloquium
that deliberately seeks to reflect the diversity and polyvalency of
contemporary gastrotexts. But it is perhaps cannibalism, one of
the last taboos in a century of virtually unrestrained
permissiveness, that focusses our attention, in the most
provocative and Absolute fashion, on the propensity of all such
discourse to illuminate the fundamental existential question of
how one engages - incorporates or rejects, absorbs or penetrates -
with others, with the Other ... Writing as Communion, an
expression newly paraclete ...

NOTES

[1] Jean-Pierre Richard, *Essai sur le romantisme*, Paris: Seuil, 1970, p. 187.
"... devouring: the primitive engorging of one being by another, then digestion,
assimilation. (...) interpenetration, taking on a cosmic significance, becomes
one of the categories of the appetite: 'All of nature that we see is eating and eaten.
The prey gnaw on each other.'"
[2] James Brown, "Littérature et Nourriture", *Dalhousie French Studies*, no. 11,
p. 5.

1.

FOOD POISONING, COOKING AND HISTORIOGRAPHY IN THE WORKS OF GÜNTER GRASS

One could claim that food, feeding and hunger - the precondition for feeding - have a pervasive presence in more or less all of Grass's prose works. These themes are least in evidence in *Aus dem Tagebuch einer Schnecke*[1] (1972; *From the Diary of a Snail*). In *Örtlich betäubt* (1969; *Local Anaesthetic*) one of the major concerns is a psychological and political presentation of the after-effects of eating, in this instance dental decay. Even *Das Treffen in Telgte* (1979; *The Meeting at Telgte*) has as one of its central events a banquet made possible by the pillaging carried out by Gelnhausen, alias Grimmelshausen. The narrative essay *Kopfgeburten oder Die Deutschen sterben aus* (1980; *Headbirths, or The Germans are dying out*), which is at the same time the equivalent of a political manifesto and is the least satisfactory of Grass's prose works, draws the attention of its readers to the fact that a large proportion of the world's populations does not have enough to eat. *Die Rättin* (1986; *The Rat*), the satiric novel which has incurred - probably justifiably - the critics' displeasure, also refers to starvation, in this instance, as a result of a nuclear explosion. Gastronomy, however, assumes its most dominant role in the Danzig trilogy, in particular in *Die Blechtrommel* (1959; *The Tin Drum*) and *Hundejahre* (1963; *Dog Years*), and also in the much later novel *Der Butt* (1977; *The Flounder*) - all of which tend to enjoy a higher esteem than the works mentioned initially. Indeed, individual and collective acts of eating abound throughout these three large novels. Eating has not merely a physical function but it also acquires a metaphorical, if not symbolical role in these works. Not unexpectedly, it extends its ramifications in order to link up with other aspects of the novels, thus vitally shaping the substance of the novels as a whole. *Die Blechtrommel*, Grass's first and probably most outstanding novel is an excellent case in point.

The role which eating assumes in the Danzig trilogy differs from its role in *Der Butt*. In the trilogy the characters, it could be

claimed, enjoy, at least superficially, the food they eat; the after-
effects, however, are in many cases wholly disagreeable, the
associations attached to the activity of eating are frequently
repulsive and the symbolical function negative. In *Der Butt* eating
is viewed from a different angle. In this instance Grass sets
himself the task of writing a history of cooks and cooking. The
attitude to cooking itself is affirmative. What emerges in this
history of women is that their lives have been marred, if not
devastated, by suffering or acts of violence. Food and feeding thus
become the positive framework within which the negative features
of German history are recorded.

Let us turn first to *Die Blechtrommel* and highlight its
gastronomic features. Even though Oskar's father is a cook, the
food that the dwarf-like child and his family have to consume often
arouses a feeling of revulsion. So frequently are characters in *Die
Blechtrommel* nauseated by the pre-war and post-war fare in
Germany that one of Grass's more abusive critics (E. Valerius)[2]
has dubbed the novel "Die Brechtrommel" ("The drum of nausea").
The physically and emotionally revolting atmosphere of the
Germany of Oskar's childhood is suggested by the scene in which
neighbouring children force-feed Oskar with a soup consisting of
bits of brick, two frogs, spittle and a dash of urine. His only
reaction is to vomit, but his desire for revenge soon finds its outlet
in destructiveness. Another act of feeding forms a prelude to his
mother's vomiting: the family watch eels devouring a horse's
head, and so nauseated is the mother that she spews the content of
her stomach onto the stones of the beach. For those who require a
visual representation of the scene Volker Schlöndorff's film of *Die
Blechtrommel* is especially expressive. The trail of vomit
continues its course through the novel to the baptism feast of
Oskar's step-brother. Here again, Oskar's gut reaction to the
mindless environment of the time assumes the form of physical
nausea. This is not to suggest that Oskar himself rebels against
his surroundings, but it is rather that he is a narrative medium
through which physical loathing may be expressed. A
particularly grotesque act of eating occurs on the occasion when
Russian soldiers enter the Matzeraths' cellar in the closing stages
of the war. Oskar's father tries to conceal his party badge - and his
party allegiance - in his mouth, that part of the body which
Matzerath the cook had tended with such loving care throughout
his life. The cook can neither swallow nor spew up, he is in
danger of choking on his badge before the Russians hasten the
process by riddling him with machine-gun bullets. Matzerath's
eating comes to a sticky end and the Nazi era comes to a close. The
demise of the person is paralleled in grotesque form by the demise

of the Nazi state. The man ceases to eat, the state ceases to gobble up Europe.

In keeping with the grotesque, the reader is tempted to laugh and cry simultaneously. One other act of eating in which Oskar indulges is a particularly fine example of the grotesque. Oskar revels in a meal of sherbet which is induced into volcanic eruption in the navel of his girlfriend on the addition of his own spittle. The incident is exceptionally amusing and yet, at the same time, this personal scene is paralleled on the political level by the violent outburst of irrationality which was characteristic of National Socialism. The highly entertaining gastronomic acrobatics of Oskar contrast with the triumph of unreason in the political realm with consequences which can only be described as tragic. As seems to be the usual pattern, food and drink are combined in communion-like manner - sherbet and spittle, cakes and coffee, beer and spaghetti or bread and wine.

The individual acts of eating - or non-eating - mentioned so far can be interpreted variously. Their transferred meaning does not neutralize their substance as part of the reality of the narrative flow. They are anchored in the down-to-earth details of the novel's world. Each act of vomiting is a gut reaction of rejection - a refusal to accept the poison of a loathsome environment. Agnes Matzerath's body in particular is convulsed with nausea at the thought of her extra-marital relationship. It is a rebellion against her own pregnancy, against the phallic emblem of eels. They have devoured the head of the horse and now they invade the body of the woman. A short time later Agnes Matzerath forces herself to eat nothing but fish, which are in plentiful supply in her husband's shop. She dies eventually of fish poisoning.

In the instances of individual eating we have mentioned so far, the rejection of poison is a frequent feature of the situation. On the other hand, there are many acts of collective eating in which the body - and by implication the body politic - absorb the poison which is administered to it. Oskar Matzerath, Grass's loyal lieutenant as narrator in *Die Blechtrommel*, describes, for example, a feast which follows the baptism of his step-brother. The guests at the meal eat their food in a mechanical and mindless manner. They spoon their soup into their mouths with the same degree of uninvolvement and passivity with which they absorb the outpourings of the Nazi propaganda machine. The constant reference to the German word "Löffel" which means both spoon and ear allows this parallel to be drawn. The body offers no resistance to the baptismal food nor to the special communiqués which form the staple diet of the German people during the war period. It is as though the German people are indulging in a collective act of communion, thereby sacrificing their individuality and their will to think otherwise.

The idea of food-poisoning is also suggested in one of the central chapters of the book which is entitled "Glaube Hoffnung Liebe" (Faith Hope and Charity). In the course of this grotesque, fairy-tale chapter the narrator relates how a gullible people comes to believe in Father Christmas, whose position is usurped in reality by the gasman. The latter announces that he is the saviour of the world without whom no cooking can take place. Built into this fairy-tale sequence are references to the Crystal Night during which Jewish synagogues and businesses were set on fire and Jews savaged or murdered. The associations with the word "gas" are developed in such a way that the double reference to physical and mental pollution gains momentum: the people prepare their food with the poison gas supplied on a national scale by the saviour of Germany, the gas is the spirit of the Holy Ghost which encompasses the minds of men and, it goes without saying, the gas is the means by which the Jews were murdered in the Nazi concentration camps.

The idea that the German people indulge in a massive communion of physical and spiritual food-poisoning is not a suggestion which occurs to the readers coincidentally: it is allusively integrated into the web of associations which form the solid substratum of the novel. A veritable banquet which Oskar and his circus companions hold on the concrete of the Atlantic fortifications in 1944 is a case in point. The communicants feast themselves on the food supplied involuntarily by the subjugated peoples of Europe and the war-time allies. Danish butter and eggs, Dutch cocoa, French plum jam, Soviet caviar, American biscuits and English corned beef are all available for the communicants. Roswitha, one of the many girl-friends with whom Oskar is amorously involved, conjures up with intentional or unintentional irony the associations of a communion meal by referring to it as a sacred act of eating which unites the peoples of the world. The bunker meal, which takes place shortly before the Allied invasion of Europe, is also the focal point for an act of barbarism in that one of the soldiers is ordered to shoot the five nuns who appear on the beach in front of the machine-gun emplacement. Communion in this instance is a prelude to brutality and accepted by the bystanders with the same degree of insensitivity with which Oskar's relatives and neighbours absorb items of war-time news.

Such a meal is re-enacted in the same place in the post-war period. Only two of the original participants are present - Oskar and Lankes, the machine-gunner. The same emotional attitudes persist and a comparable barbaric act is committed - Lankes rapes a nun who then proceeds to drown herself. The fish which is the main ingredient of the picnic launches the two men into a dispute as to who should have the head and who the tail. Allusively the dispute is one between reason and passion. To judge by Lankes's subsequent behaviour, it is the principle of irrationality which emerges triumphant. The communicants who gather together on these two occasions for a meal on the Atlantic fortifications celebrate not the principle of reason, or love and compassion, but the principle of unreason and unbridled emotion.

There are other occasions where the narrator allows correspondences to emerge between a particular meal and the idea of communion and the conventions associated with it. One such example is the scene in Schmuh's Onion Cellar, a rather bizarre night-club. Here Schmuh, the proprietor, acts out the daily role of High Priest and distributes "onion flesh" to the attenders, who are then enabled to weep the tears of contrition otherwise denied them because of their incapacity to mourn. There are also specific occasions in the novel when direct references are made to bread and wine, those elements which are the indispensable items in the celebration of communion. A Black Mass, for example, is celebrated in the latter stages of the war with Oskar acting out the role of Christ and Antichrist, and with the so-called Dusters, a Danzig set of hooligans, constituting the congregation. One of the Dusters, acting as priest, administers the bread and wine, and to the accompaniment of Oskar's drum, the words "This is my body" are pronounced. This parody of the Eucharist indicates the extent to which religion has been disembowelled and usurped by paganism and anarchism. An act of eating and drinking has provided the basis for sanctifying the childish egocentricity of Oskar.

One further parody of the communion occurs in the final chapter of the book in which Oskar is arrested and then transferred to a mental asylum. He pronounces his personal credo, concluding it by referring to the "Black Cook", a female figure of dread who haunts Oskar's mind and drives him to insanity. The "Cook" is clearly a figment of a childish imagination and is a means by which Oskar retreats voluntarily, or is thrust involuntarily, into madness. It embodies Oskar's fear of woman and his terror of being poisoned by the food she may force upon him. Born into the world by the sexual act of a cook, Oskar withdraws from the adult world pursued by a woman representative of those women cooks who in the course of his career have compelled him, like temptresses, to absorb or vomit their venom.

In *Katz und Maus* references to eating - and to communion - are much less frequent and do not really make an indispensable contribution to the totality of the *novella*. And yet, in one particularly distinctive scene, Mahlke, whose legendary exploits form the substance of the narrative, consumes frogs' legs from a rusty tin which he had salvaged from the submerged hulk of a wrecked submarine, thereby causing one of his schoolmates to spew up in the direction of the harbour entrance. Moreover, to some degree it could even be claimed that the central imagery of the *novella* is dependent in effect on an act of eating. Mahlke, the schoolboy who becomes a tank commander, suffers from a huge inferiority complex which has its origins in his oversized Adam's apple. His school companions inadvertently draw his attention to this defect by placing a cat on his throat. The animal, attracted by the movements of the larynx, plays with it as though it were a mouse. Mahlke tries to divert attention from it by indulging in all manner of exhibitionism, whether within the school environment or on the field of war. The mouse sticks in Mahlke's throat, he is unable to swallow it (and digest it) or spew it up and hence rid his body - and his mind - of an obstacle to his mental harmony. If the Adam's apple is likened to a mouse, then it follows that Mahlke may be viewed as the cat, though other recipients for the title can be found in the story. Like Alfred Matzerath, Joachim Mahlke chokes on an object in his throat. His life founders on an act of eating which miscarries.

Hundejahre, the third member of the Danzig trilogy, has much in common with *Die Blechtrommel* in that references to eating form a pattern of associations which suggest on a metaphorical level the contamination of body and mind characteristic of National Socialism. The novel, which consists of three books, has three authors to correspond to these three sections. The three authors, the Jew Eddie Amsel, Harry Liebenau and Walter Matern, together with a girl by the name of Tulla Pokriefke, form the human framework within which the novel unfolds. There is one other character of central importance to the novel, the dog whose bestiality increases as the novel progresses. The book describes that period of time, especially the Nazi era, when Germany and the Germans went to the dogs. The dog, which is a black Alsatian - a German sheep-dog - has a central position in the novel because of its relationship to the narrative. What enhances its significance is the fact that interconnections are frequently made between Hitler and the dog. Events in the life of the Alsatian are placed side by side with events which are linked directly or indirectly with Hitler. A German sheep-dog, for example, is presented to the Führer by the people of Danzig, and when Harry Liebenau and his father are summoned as representative citizens into the Führer's presence, it is not Hitler they meet but the dog, Prinz. We learn that one of the dog's close ancestors is descended from a Lithuanian she-wolf and had to be destroyed because it reverted to type. Such associations, the correspondences with Hitler and the potential savagery of the animal, are enhanced when one of the dogs, the sire of Hitler's dog, does in reality savage a local pianist, on two occasions egged on by Tulla. The latter, who acts out the role of a vicious and insidious temptress, spends seven days living with the dog in its kennel. As a sign of her degeneration to an animal-like level, she eats the dog's meat. The nauseating scene is described in much detail: Harry Liebenau takes a bowl of offal to the kennel, makes the usual whistling and hissing noises as though he were trying to attract the dog, rather than Tulla. After Harry has left the bowl behind, Tulla emerges from the kennel on all fours, removes the layer of fat from the bowl and sickeningly drinks the contents. We also learn that Tulla, her brothers and Harry Liebenau have all at one stage or another eaten the dog's meat, and after such a meal they all begin to behave as though they had been transformed into dogs, speaking differently and almost barking at each other. It is clear that such acts of eating have symbolical undertones: Tulla - and the children - eat the meat of a dog, which is capable of savagery, is in imminent danger of reverting to its wolf-like habits and which is likened to the personality of the Führer. The children eat the meal as a sign of their spiritual bondage. Such an act echoes the communion service - they are eating the flesh of their master.

The children engage in another activity which demonstrates in image form how Tulla is attempting to poison the small community of which she is a dominant member. If the main ingredient of Tulla's meal of dog food is flesh, then the main ingredient of this second example is blood. In this sense both acts of eating are reminiscent of communion. From her headquarters in the swan house which is likened to the dog's kennel, Tulla directs the collecting of the leeches which three of them, Tulla, Jenny and Harry, have to attach to their bodies. The leeches, once they have sucked their fill of blood, are boiled in water over a small fire until they burst. The children then have to drink this gory concoction ("Suppe" - soup - is one of the words which is used and reminds the reader of similar equally nauseating acts of drinking and eating in *Die Blechtrommel*). Tulla considers boiling leeches to be sacred, and by stating this she allows the reader to draw an analogy between this act of drinking blood and the communion service during which the blood of Christ is drunk. To encourage the participation of the other children in her pseudo-religious observances, she reminds them that the Jew Eddie Amsel and his friend Walter Matern were blood-brothers. As in the Church's ritual they feel themselves to be united - or contaminated spiritually - like blood brothers. Tulla has infested the blood of her contemporaries - she has engaged in sanguinary "Gleichschaltung".

A third act of eating (and boiling) takes place in the Sawatzkis' home after the end of the war. Inge and Jochen Sawatzki make syrup from sugar beet whilst Matern watches the proceedings. The three of them celebrate the creed of amnesia in this communion-like activity rather than their spiritual allegiance to Christ and God, the sweetness of their product sentimentally clouding their minds with forgetfulness. As in *Die Blechtrommel*, eating and drinking in *Hundejahre* evoke the emotional climate within people whose minds have been drugged into insensitivity and into tolerating - and executing - acts of bestiality. In both those works of the Danzig trilogy the associations connected with communion are conjured up and become a means of indicating how the minds of the Germans are contaminated by the insidious atmosphere of their times. In *Die Blechtrommel* the adherents of the Nazi regime are depicted as benefiting from Hitler's campaign against hunger and cold, and revelling in their own gluttony. In so doing they prove themselves to be political romantics, victims of their voracious appetites because of their inability to come to terms with the present, and accordingly they fill their minds with dreams of the future. Klepp, whose form of communion consists in a constant allegiance to beer and spaghetti, maintains that dreamers are gluttons, and the characters in the novel confirm the correctness of this opinion. The gormandizing of the individual is paralleled on the national level by the political ambitions of an imperialistic Germany which tries to gobble up Europe in attempting to satisfy its expansionistic aspirations. The greediness of the individual symbolizes the insatiable appetite of the German national state. Inordinate appetite, however, leads to catastrophe. What applies to Agnes Matzerath and her lover, Jan Bronski, applies equally to the Germans and Germany at large: "Die hatten den großen Appetit, der nie aufhört, der sich selbst in den Schwanz beißt."[3]

In a general sense it may be claimed that the treatment of the theme of communion contributes, in both *Die Blechtrommel* and *Hundejahre*, to the all-pervading atmosphere of debunking. Grass enjoys the process of knocking standard values - in this case of a religious nature - unceremoniously from the pedestals they have been occupying for centuries. Grass's handling of communion is an example of what M. Hodgart[4] refers to as "desymbolisation". At the same time he is demonstrating how religious values and religious customs have been hollowed out, deprived of any moral content and debased to a purely pagan level.

In *Der Butt* eating and drinking are not employed as a vast image to suggest the spiritual contamination of a whole people. Grass is concerned rather to write a history of food and of cooking. In collecting material for this venture the author became aware of women's anonymous contribution to history and this realization was accompanied by the discovery of Grimm's fairy-story "Vom Fischer und seiner Frau" ("The Fisherman and his Wife"). A third element was provided by the birth of a daughter to Grass's wife. Though Grimm's fairy-tale and the birth of a child enjoy parity of esteem with the cooks, the history of cooks and cooking provides the chronological sequence in the novel and is at the same time a history of the sexes, of the emancipation of man from woman and of woman from man - a survey of history which is the counterpart to the official version presented in the text books. The cooks provide an additional cohesive element within the book in that food and recipes are constant ingredients within the novel, and each of the nine parts - one for each month of the pregnancy - contains one chapter or at least the conclusion of a chapter in which a meal is described.

Even in the first short paragraph of the novel the themes to which we have just referred are rapidly drawn to the attention of the reader. Admittedly a reference to the fish is not included, but the wife of the author-cum-narrator is called Ilsebill, which is the name of the fisher's wife in Grimm's fairy-tale: "Ilsebill salzte nach. Bevor gezeugt wurde, gab es Hammelschulter zu Bohnen und Birnen, weil Anfang Oktober. Beim Essen noch, mit vollem Mund sagte sie: 'Wollen wir nun gleich ins Bett oder willst du mir vorher erzählen, wie unsere Geschichte wann wo begann?'"[5] Thus the themes of eating, procreation - as the prelude to the birth of a daughter - and history make their entrance onto Grass's stage in a startling and amusing manner, and usher in a pageant of cooks and associated characters, many of whom act in accordance with the advice of the speaking fish.

In the second chapter of the book - still within the first month of pregnancy - we are introduced to Grass's representative cooks and we are provided with a potted version of their characters and lives. The narrator, who has been granted nine months - the parts or subsections of the book - to give birth to his cooks, allocates each cook to a specific period of time. He delves back into the beginnings of time and then ranges far and wide over the course of history, including the Stone Age, the Iron Age, the Tenth Century, the Gothic Age, the Reformation, the Thirty Years' War, the Eighteenth Century with its introduction of the potato into Prussia, the age of the French Revolution, the Franco-Prussian War, the two World Wars and, finally, the sixties of this century in both Germany and Poland. Each cook is portrayed as a projection of Ilsebill, the wife of the narrator-cum-author, into the past, and each man with whom the cook associates is the narrator in a different guise. In short, each narrator and each cook are united by the bonds of food - and sex.

In the course of this historical survey the narrator-cum-author is at pains to highlight the fact that violence has been a dominant factor in many of the lives and deaths of the cooks. The novel is in effect an indictment of man's inhumanity to man - and to woman. In this sense the two novels, *Die Blechtrommel* and *Der Butt*, come to similar conclusions, but by different routes. In *Die Blechtrommel* food and eating are employed as metaphorical weapons in the denunciation of man. In *Der Butt* cooks and cooking are the framework within which man's extremism may be exposed. One obvious difference between the two novels is that *Der Butt* covers a much longer time span than the earlier novel, whilst *Die Blechtrommel* deals merely with the years from 1899 to 1954, with the main emphasis on the Nazi and postwar period.

Der Butt comes to a further conclusion which it shares with *Die Blechtrommel*. Man's boundless ambitions have brought death and destruction to his fellow human beings. Man in his various guises has been and is as insatiable as the fisher in the unofficial version of the fairy-tale. Both man and woman are equally voracious in the demands they make, in their hunger for things material and spiritual, and thus the appetite that can never be satisfied has brought war and catastrophe to the world. The connection between the craving for food and the yearning for material possessions and power is not made explicit. However, the effects of physical hunger on a global scale are made clear: starvation is as brutal in its effect as are the wars occasioned by man's ambition to conquer the world and nature. The narrator himself claims that the hunger which affects large areas of the world is also a form of war. In one of the narrator's many guises, that of Vasco da Gama, he suggests that he ought to write a history of hunger either as an addition to, or instead of the present work. Both novels adopt a similar attitude to history. Both works convey a sense of horror at man's lack of moderation and his irrationality. They both present a statement of account, a historical survey which takes the form of a lament. In *Der Butt* in particular, history is portrayed as a kind of treadmill which, with sickening regularity, allows circumstances and situations to recur whose basic similarity is not obscured by superficial differences. History is a constant process of regurgitation. In *Die Blechtrommel* the theme of circularity is conveyed through the image of the roundabout. Interlinking all historical events - whether in monumental happenings or in the lives of the cooks in *Der Butt* or of the characters in *Die Blechtrommel* - is the continuous thread of violence. Günter Grass achieves this historical overview - or perhaps underview might be a more appropriate term - by exploiting the imagery of eating and drinking in *Die Blechtrommel* and *Hundejahre* and by elaborating on the personal and social history of cooks in *Der Butt*.

Noel Thomas

NOTES

[1] The prose works of Günter Grass are published in hardback and paperback by Hermann Luchterhand Verlag, Darmstadt and Neuwied. They have been translated into English by Ralph Manheim and are published by Penguin Books.

[2] E. Valerius, "Giftzwerg Oskar rührt die blasphemische Brechtrommel. Zu Günter Grass: *Die Blechtrommel*", *Das Neue Journal*, Wiesbaden, Vol. 8, 1960, No. 5, pp. 33-35.

[3] "They had the ravenous appetite that never dies down, that bites its own tail." (translation by Ralph Manheim, *The Tin Drum*, p. 97).

[4] Matthew Hodgart, *Satire*, London: Weidenfeld and Nicolson, 1969, p. 123.

[5] "Ilsebill put on more salt. Before the impregnation there was shoulder of mutton with string beans and pears, the season being early October. Still at table, still with her mouth full, she asked, 'Should we go to bed right away, or do you first want to tell me how when where our story began?'" (translated by Ralph Manheim, Penguin Books).

2.

FAST FOOD/QUICK LUNCH: CREWS, BURROUGHS AND PYNCHON

Bye, Bye, Miss American Pie
(Don MacLean)

Si l'écart qui fait, des deux
lèvres, la différence sensible
ne peut jamais être réduit,
encore moins effacé, l'écart
qui sépare la bouche de l'objet
qui apaisera son désir peut,
lui, être réduit jusqu'à
l'annulation de toute distance.
(Serge Leclaire)[1]

Exuberant, gross and grim, peculiarly American tall tales of old carnival hands trace a wonderland map of lost highways, forbidden pleasures on which the sexual drive is accompanied by road, food and the continuous chance to involve oneself with death. French fried in Freud, this American joy of cooking might be understood as suppression of the distance between a mouth and its desire, a need made possible by the sensitive, felt difference between two lips which can never be completely erased. This is the temporary fix, the insertion of any object which, in its density, texture, opacity and palpable substance, takes the place of an irreducible, originary lack. This is the place of an unread, lost letter, the marker on the borders of past bliss, the access to an erogenous zone. They can be traced anywhere, yet manifest themselves most easily where orifices gape, pucker, squeeze, pinch or suck to close that impossible distance, that minuscule gap in grip, clench or touch. If, as Serge Leclaire suggests, there is an essential alterity implied in the conception of the erogenous body, then its organization can only sustain itself by a fundamental otherness in relation to a missing term.[2] In an American context, one in which systems of opposition and identification are privileged, a relation with otherness is eschewed in favour of "eating the Other". This confrontational stance breaks relations into things, digitalizes them in competition and challenge, into a desire for obstacle. Preoccupation with performance, with appetite, with its stimulation or suppression, as Anthony Wilden points out,[3] with mind/body dualism, makes for a reification of both. Fear of losing desire without the obstacle makes for that special sadness, the uninvited guest at every American repast, whether righteous or aberrant.

That which is at the end of the fork, the "naked lunch" of forked creatures, is addiction to that piece, part, part-object which simultaneously guarantees the place of lack even as it momentarily hides it, closing the distance between "mouth" and "food". But any place on the bodily envelope can be a secret hearth, on which can be rekindled or re-marked an anticipation of pleasure, a tension of yearning, a drooling which the stuffing of bliss can only momentarily relieve. Short of death, of eternal unconsciousness, any bit, piece, lump, chunk, morsel or bite will do, to suck, chew and hold. The nourishment in question having nothing to do with a homeostasis of health or with the organism's survival. It is pleasure which cannot be reduced to organic function. It feeds the dream of power and peace with which the atomized individual engulfs the world and all its separate things.

This is as American as, well, apple pie and Chevrolet, see the USA in your ..., or as "Miss Budweiser", the hydroplane reaching the vertigo of forbidden limits. Cold wedges wait in the Automat, the promised Miss or missing piece, waiting just a while longer, while the rocket overhead passes the last delta-t. Twilight in America before the Reagan hangover, "Miller Time", cars and songs in carefully orchestrated retro-periodization. Television's "Crime Story" has artifacts from the nineteen-fifties, and the commercial spot for Wendy's Classic has old cars featured in the show, seemingly eaten as hamburgers and sold in a box that looks like an old sealed-beam headlight.

Harry Crews's *Car*, of 1972, takes place in the south, specifically the car-culture south, in which the whole food-chain of automobile consumption, from buying to modifying, crashing, junking and compressing for scrap metal, punctuates the lives of the characters and writes on their flesh. Cars figure in their dreams, sexual initiations, their joy and their pain, indispensable partners in their imaginary fixations.

The stunt of a man attempting to eat a car cut up into small chunks by an acetylene torch, smoothed, sterilised, padded in bread, so that it can move on through the digestive tract and bowel to land in a plate, is described in the most painful detail, from indigestion to the anal haemorrhaging which obliges him to abandon his goal. Carnival barkers sell seats so that Herman Mack on his throne, his *chaise percée*, can pass the car's bits while in front of an audience, pieces which are then sold to the highest bidder, fragments of a Ford which have passed through a human being. These heterogeneous elements, swallowed one by one, constitute the carapace of car, container of the American monad *par excellence*. This grotesque homage, an ultimately impossible one, is nonetheless a poignant and logical tribute.

To write of the pleasure of eating is to observe the conventions of the gourmet's text: words that would signal intimate caresses of the palate, the throat's convulsive satisfaction. This written enjoyment is framed by unseen recipes for dizzying nausea, soul-shaking retching, voluptuous heaving, overpowering and involuntary expulsions of abhorrent fare. That is, unless the gag reflex can be circumvented, a skill acquired by the prostitute who falls for the hero. She understands his ordeal and recalls her first dates and their cars, as he, bloated and bleeding, swallows the unrecognizable metal lumps of the object itself. He acts out, accepts literally the invitations "to eat" implied incessantly in the mass media's will to colonize internal eco-systems with the edible and the inedible. This is done through images that would anchor the Imaginary in an apogee of consumption, of slaked thirst and sated hunger. Outside the tube's technicolor feeding-trough of exemplary consumption, beyond satiation, is a desperate re-sensitizing of irreducible difference, the forbidden limits of addiction. The mouth's pleasure and the mind's escape lead to fatal excesses, revealing the incompatibility, indeed the opposition, between enjoyment and health.

Thomas Pynchon's *Gravity's Rainbow*, of 1973, is seasoned with incorrigibly sophomoric provocations which break up the forbidding metaphysical speculations of the novel with limericks, puns, terrible jokes, and a feast for the eye of gross delights. There is the "disgusting English candy drill",[4] during which Tyrone Slothrop is urged to sample the most surprisingly disagreeable flavours and unsettling combinations of ingredients, the foreign adventure's rites of passage over plate and palate. But even as moist reception centres gingerly palpate alien morsels, however inert or smooth, it is the words that finally bring to life the unthinkable.

During an elaborate meal in the Zone, in chaotic Germany

immediately after her defeat in WWII, rebels and free spirits who thrive in suspension of normal life find themselves sitting down with those who will quickly rationalize and routinize the postwar economy, in effect, cannibalize marginal undesirables. Noting with alarm *Ueberraschungbraten*, surprise roast, on the menu, they are quick to devise a stratagem, serious silliness that will nauseate their hosts, disperse the guests, and play for time. There follows a shouting out of fondly reminisced "delicacies", favourite dishes not part of the elaborate meal before them. This is an exorcism of fear through hilarious camaraderie, poisonous, malodorous recipes for nausea, which sneer at the viscous evidence of mortality the human mollusc exudes. As if, too, to eat our slimy trail, the soft ooze of nightmarish nutrition, would be a fitting remembrance of the carnage and genocide which fed the monstrous appetite of the just-ended war. The war of words at table throws up menace in defiant declamation, compiled here in order of their appearance during the calculated revelry:

snot soup	vegetables venereal slobber sauce
smegna stew	wart waffles
scum soufflé	puke pancakes with seat syrup
menstrual marmalade	pinworm preserves
clot casserole	hemorrhoid hash
afterbirth appetizers	bowel burgers
scab sandwiches	leprosy loaf
booger biscuits	gangrene goulash
mucus mayonnaise	fungus fricassee
slime sausage	nosepick noodles
discharge dumplings	grime gruel
canker consommé	pustule porridge
barf bouillon	carbuncle cutlets
vomit vichyssoise	groin gravy
cyst salad	ringworm relish
fart fudge	crotch custard
boil blintzes	phlegm fudge
	mold muffins

Typically, Pynchon's characters burst into song as the party breaks up:

> Oh gimme some o' that acne, à la mode,
> Eat so much - that Ah, jes'explode!
> Say there buddih you can chow all nite, on
> Toe-jam tarts 'n Diarrhea Dee-lite ...[5]

The hidden other mouth that all share, the last defenceless

border between the self and the Other, through which life seems to pass into waste, is as well the symbol of universal tender, the transformation of everything into capital. Inseparable from war, the smell of shit is indigenous to love and to the precious bonding between the living and dying that persists in the slaughter of combat.

So it is that Pynchon's Brigadier Pudding arranges to relive the paroxysms of the Great War in coprophilia, to ingest again, to transgress the limits of revulsion:

> The stink of shit floods his nose, gathering him, surrounding. It is the smell of Passchendaele, of the Salient. Mixed with mud and the putrefaction of corpses, it was the sovereign smell of their first meeting, and her emblem. The turd slides into his mouth, down to his gullet. He gags, but bravely clamps his teeth shut. Bread that only would have floated in porcelain waters somewhere unseen, untasted - risen now and baked in the bitter intestinal Oven to bread we know, bread that's light as domestic comfort, secret as death in bed.[6]

From the courage building of boys in barracks and locker-room, to tragic and morbid rites, the Other as challenge and obstacle, as distance to be traversed on a dare, is privileged fare.

Fear of "rancid ectoplasm" is dear to William Burroughs, as are images of liquefaction that torment the junky in his terrible need, before he "cooks up" a shot. Burroughs's prophetic *Naked Lunch* of 1959 seems to have been a kind of enabling act without which the likes of Pynchon, Crews and others would be difficult to imagine.[7] It is precisely in Burroughs's exploration of the forbidden that a new American frontier is established, just in time for the experience of drugs and war during the cultural revolution of the sixties, and later, the struggle between analgesia and addiction, the substance abuse of the eighties.

Burroughs's "voice" is that of a side-show impresario, an ageing mischievous "good old boy", with a put-on gravelly drawl, coming from a poker-faced husk chuckling in phlegm, savouring blackest of humour. It was to become the "sorry about that" grim apology for "just desserts" of jellied gasoline or phosphorous custard thrown indiscriminately, "home cooking" courtesy of the Dow Chemical Company, whose sanctimonious advertising today makes gorges rise.

For Burroughs, "eating the Other" is a *rendez-vous* with
inelastic need, a satisfaction so absolute as to turn the addict into a
thing. It becomes as well the premonition of future mutations that
would shuck off the rotting bodies' prison for an electric escape.
Pynchon, too, worries about "Control", wonders whose dreams we
service and host, who is colonizing our intimate surfaces as we
relax our throats to receive? One man's succulence is another's
offal, but increasingly, involuntarily, the "secret self" is pleasured
by a commodity aesthetics of unrelenting aggression and
sophistication, renaming the anchoring points of the imaginary
with the sign posts of corporate trademarks. Amidst incessant
"appetite emergencies", glistening bodies at workout or on the
construction site, we jerk to the rap master's beat, his staccato
invitations to ingest, indulge, resist or refrain: "This Bud's for
you!" "Say No to drugs!". The tension the performance principle
exacts is what energizes the consumer, who twitches to a binary
on/off of fix and need, quantified gratification that is fuel-injected
and computer-controlled, leaving behind the needle tracks of the
digital.

Chiquita Banana's phallus arches over *Gravity's Rainbow*
from the beginning of the novel, when roof-top banana plants in
wartime London are harvested for a succulent breakfast, to the end
of the novel, in America, when bananas are discovered in a
refrigerator. Her fruit represents the work as a whole: the
rocket's thrust and fall, tumescent life threatened by the planet's
despoliation through ruthless ordering of a technology that will
embalm or incinerate us all. Addiction to the rocket, to
destruction, to a sterile vision of frozen fixity seems to be winning
out over breakfast's optimism:

> Now there grows among all the rooms, replacing the
> night's old smoke, alcohol and sweat, the fragile
> musaceous odor of breakfast, flowery, permeating,
> surprising, more than the color of winter sunlight,
> taking over ... by the high intricacy to the weaving of its
> molecules, sharing the conjuror's secret by which ... the
> living genetic chains prove even labyrinthine enough to
> preserve some human face down ten twenty generations
> ... so the same assertion-through-structure allows this
> war morning's banana fragrance to meander,
> repossess and prevail.[8]

This is contrasted with what Pynchon calls "ice boxery: freezing
back the tumultuous cycles of the day to preserve this odorless
small world, this cube of changelessness".[9] The discovery of

bananas in there, "bananas! who-who's been putting bananas - in-
the-refrigerator! O non-no-no, no-no-no! Chiquita Banana sez we
shouldn't! Somethin' awful'll happen! Who would do that?"[10]
Chiquita's appearance in the last pages of *Gravity's Rainbow* is
ominous; the recent revival of the jingle is even more so to Pynchon
fans. In the October 20, 1986 issue of *New York*, it was noted that:

> Chiquita Banana has resurrected its forty-one year old
> jingle. "The nostalgia craze drove us back to our
> classic advertising jingle," admits Dennis Werner,
> Vice-president of Marketing for Chiquita bananas.
> "But we were also picking up that an awful lot of people
> out there once they heard the Chiquita name, would
> break into the old song 'I'm Chiquita Banana and I've
> come to say ...'. Our goal was to keep people thinking of
> Chiquita and bananas as hand in hand. It's an image
> campaign like what IBM would run."

Years ago, United Fruit's saucy promotion had set off fevered
imaginations with:

> I'm Chiquita Banana and I've come to say
> I come from little island down equator way
> I sail on big banana boat from Caribe
> to see if I can help good neighbor policy.
> I bring a song about bananas
> I sing it low, I sing it high,
> I make big hit with 'mericanos
> singing song about bananos.
> I could sing about the moonlight
> on the very very tropical equator
> but no I sing about bananas and the
> refrigerator, si si si si.

In Pynchon's words, they were "masturbatory fantasies of nailing
this cute but older Latin lady *while she's wearing her hat*, gigantic
fruit-market hat, and a big saucy smile".[11]

In *Car*, the prostitute shows the car-eating hero her room
filled with strap-on dildoes; in *Naked Lunch*, the "banana" turns
out to be a strap-on as well, Steely Dan by name. And today,
outside in the "real world", Chiquita carries a Kalishnikov
automatic rifle with its distinctive "banana" clip, while Honduras
has become a garrison state on the Empire's frontier.

Product loyalty wavers, the "American Pie" has become, in
Hillman and Boer's *Freud's Own Cookbook*, a Pynchonesque

"paranoid Pie", for they warn us that "cyanide smells like almonds", and urge we bake it again "to kill the bacteria".[12] Indeed, unthinkable insertions, ingestions, exchanges of bodily fluids haunt appetites in *fin-de-siècle* America, even as frenzied efforts are made to colonize every private rim, to bring back Josephine Baker and Chiquita, to peel it and pop it in!

Burroughs has shown how the promotion of addiction, cooking up "joy" in a "loving spoonful", is the most efficient way of passing over and out of the din. But it goes on: the dots of the TV grid prick between the eyelids, stitch their solicitation to close the gap with food, cars and carnage - after the Libyan bombing, Khadafi exclaims, "I didn't order those pizzas!". With the gag reflex circumvented it all goes down, and out. For to pinch off the stool, bite through the crust, tilt the bottle, is to switch channels, tickle the "remote commander", feed the eye as well. We ingest and pass to an electronic beat, sorting faster and faster, like Maxwell's Demon, to avoid entropic constipation or the "odd unstomachable meal". So the surface of pizza fades into the twisted rubble and flesh of a car bombing, the telltale escape of gases around the O-ring are mimicked by the coffee-maker's hisses of steam, and the end of the rainbow threatens to become *bananes flambées*.

What is needed are recipes interminable, and taking more time to chew. But outside, endless lines of Butor's ice-cream-coloured cars wait, prayer beads of a faltering economy. So alike they are and so interchangeable, that only their names mark the place, the need they must assuage. Lumps of metal, glass, plastic and rubber become dreams of escape, of final encapsulation. If only we could eat them, pass them, do it on warm leatherette, take the food to go and spill it on those very same seats, as the tyres bite and the engine "comes on cam". In the Imaginary's struggles to achieve the traction of a desired "oneness", it turns to an especially American embodiment of it, receding now in the retro-periodization of a nineteen fifties' adolescence: Ford vs. Chevy in the Big Boy drive-in parking lot, the taste of mayonnaise sauce smeared on the wheel as the V-8's rumble. "Eat it! Eat my dust!" we used to taunt, and the forbidden meals of those innocent days came and went, but never closed the gap of pleasure remembered. Hidden behind the violence of bristling jeers, jokes, boasts, jibes and menacing objects - all toys of a homo-social world - vulnerability is infinitely, tenderly protective of a secret surrender it would postpone until death itself.

Sanford Ames

NOTES

[1] Serge Leclaire, *Psychanalyser*, Paris: Seuil, 1968, p. 80.

[2] Ibid., p. 82.

[3] Anthony Wilden, *System and Structure: Essays in Communication and Exchange*, New York: Tavistock /Methuen, 1980, p. 71.

[4] Thomas Pynchon, *Gravity's Rainbow*, New York: Viking Press, 1973, pp. 116-9.

[5] Ibid., pp.714-7.

[6] Ibid., pp. 235-6.

[7] William Burroughs, *The Naked Lunch*, Paris: Olympic Press, 1959.

[8] *Gravity's Rainbow*, p. 10.

[9] Ibid., p. 678.

[10] Ibid.

[11] Ibid.

[12] James Hillman and Charles Boer, *Freud's Own Cookbook*, New York: Harper and Row, 1985.

3.

VIRGINIA WOOLF'S "BOEUF EN DAUBE"

Is it an irony that one of the most important sequences in Virginia Woolf's novel, *To the Lighthouse* (1927), should focus on food when the author herself frequently had to be coaxed to eat? Not really, since Woolf was not dealing with ordinary beef, vegetables, and fruits, but these ingredients as depicted in the work of art. Influenced by the concepts of the French impressionists and Cézanne, while also using the stream-of-consciousness method, she transmuted the objects of her awareness into the written word. Food, then, was not to be ingested through the mouth, but rather through intricate visual and psychological patternings presented to the reader by means of form, composition, mass, line, pigmentation, and shading of light and dark. Woolf's visual approach to writing allowed her to connect the disparate, give shape to the chaotic, and depict past, present, and future in unwinding patterns.

Aesthetic reasons were not solely responsible for Woolf's adoption of impressionism and Cézannism as literary techniques. Psychological considerations also influenced her. In that Woolf was what in Jungian terms is known as "a feeling and intuitive type," we may suggest that her thinking function was underdeveloped, she projected the contents of her unconscious on what she saw and experienced. For Woolf, then, both the impressionists and Cézanne fulfilled a psychic need: the impressionists answered the requirements of her feeling function, and her study of Cézanne helped her develop the primitive thinking sphere within her psyche.

The protagonist of *To the Lighthouse*, the still beautiful fifty-year-old Mrs Ramsay, the mother of eight children, stands out as a protective, sympathetic, and compassionate person. She is forever looking for ways in which to cushion life's abrasions for others. She thinks and senses in terms of the natural world of which she is a part. Neither hyper-emotional nor overly affective, her judgments depend upon her feelings. *She feels what she is*, is aware of her characteristics and attributes, and is thus in harmony with herself and the part she plays in life. It is important for her to love and to know that she is loved in return. To her family and friends, Mrs Ramsay seems to be goodness incarnate. The colours in which she is portrayed are usually white, grey, and blue; the designs drawn by Woolf to reflect her mood are circles and curves.

Although Mrs Ramsay leaves her home, stepping into an unframed exterior space, to do her marketing, visiting, or simply to look at the lighthouse across the bay, she spends most of her time within a circumscribed world. A paradigm of the feminine universe, it is the family unit that counts for her, and it is within this domain, a repository for a certain kind of wisdom, that the "dinner" she prepares enters the sphere of the work of art.

Mrs Ramsay's "dinner" is of such significance to her that it may also be said to take on the power and dimension of a religious ritual. It begins with a preparation (prelude), continues with family and friends (congregation) assembling to partake in the meal (communion) that leads to celestial configurations, and ends with the return into the earthly sphere. In each of the sequences, Woolf manipulates her visual images by interconnecting ideas and feelings on dramatic emotional planes as well as in cool or hot tones, accenting or diminishing them in accordance with the mood of the moment.

The prelude: Mrs Ramsay with two of her children are in her bedroom. She is getting dressed for dinner, and she encourages them to select the right jewelry for her to wear. The children open her jewelry box, remove much of its contents, and strew the jewelry about in the excitement of making a choice. The disorder within is suddenly paralleled by that of the rooks outside. Attempting to find a tree upon which to settle, the birds fly here and there, chirping, rising "up into the air" and down again, dissatisfied, trying to decide on the best branch on which to alight.

Mrs Ramsay presently goes down to dinner, her attitude is regal as she accepts the silent plaudits of those gathered below as a

> ... tribute to her beauty... like some queen who, finding
> her people gathered in the hall, looks down upon them,
> and descends among them, and acknowledges their
> tributes silently, and accepts their devotion and their
> prostration before her.[1]

The congregation: Mrs Ramsay is now installed at the head of the table like those ancient masters of ceremonies, the priests, handing out the Host and the wine. The archetypal mother exists on both a personal and a transpersonal plane, in the moment as well as in eternity: "She had a sense of being past everything."[2] The table may be looked upon as an altar and the plates on it, like "white circles", as mandalas or Hosts; each plate - standing individually and in group formation - represents life's continuity, a harmony of contraries. As paradigms for the Host, the plates may be considered mysterious forces, essences that flow into an individual at the height of Communion and provoke feelings of ecstasy during the Mass, when all present are engulfed in a single and unique experience.

The evening meal is "the culmination of a life" for Mrs Ramsay; it is an *agape*, during which each person present will enter a blessed area and there experience a sense of sharing and belonging. Yet, as Mrs Ramsay looks down the table, she wonders whether her life has amounted merely to "ladling out soup". She sees her husband, seated at the opposite end of the table, and feels his moodiness; emotional vibrations of other sorts momentarily encircle her, weigh her down. She looks at the old Augustus Carmichael, the lyric poet, at Charles Tansley, at Mr Bankes, and at Lily, all friends of the family: "They all sat separate. And the whole of the effort of merging and flowing and creating rested on her."[3] Mrs Ramsay realises that she is the nurturing maternal force, the unifying power that bestows collective existence on those within her orbit, allowing each to relate to others and to him- or herself. She is mother, wife, friend; she is provider of understanding, sympathy, and compassion. Nevertheless, as archetypal mother, she is alone.

Lily, a painter, focuses her thoughts meanwhile not only on the ceremony of the family dinner that will shortly begin, but also on a canvas she is in the process of completing. Withdrawing into her interior world, she questions herself about the perspective and unity - or lack of these - that she hopes to instill into her painting. "Yes, I shall put the tree further in the middle; then I shall avoid that awkward space."[4] To remind herself to move the tree, she takes up the salt-cellar and puts it down on a budding flower in the pattern of the tablecloth. Her choice of salt-cellar as a mnemonic device is not surprising. It stands out from its surroundings, not unlike the lighthouse, in its vertical spatiality and concrete upright shape. It also represents an abstract and philosophical notion: that of a tree as axis and that of salt as wisdom. Salt preserves and destroys through corrosion - hence, if the upright

tree were misplaced, its effect would be negative. For Christ, salt
was a purifying force (Matt. 5:13); it was used in the ritual of
baptism and spells spiritual nourishment.   If one partakes of
bread and salt, fraternity and consociation result.

Lily's eyes shift back to the others at the table. She observes
the silences and the idle chatter, and Mrs Ramsay who "pitied
men always as if they lacked something - women never, as if they
had something."[5] Her thoughts drift off again to her canvas:
"There's the sprig on the tablecloth; there's my painting; I must
move the tree to the middle; that matters - nothing else."[6] Lily
suddenly feels as if she is sitting among opposing energy patterns,
each personality conflicting with the others.   She probes the
essence of being "as in an x-ray photograph."[7] Her eye catches a
fixed point on the tablecloth, the salt-cellar, a paradigm of the tree
in her painting as well as of the lighthouse - imponderables. Both
objects come to life in her mind, giving her the impression of form,
density, and mass.   The interstices of white amid the floral
designs fill Lily with accentuated rhythmic sensations as if she
were floating on water to the lighthouse. The floral design recedes
briefly as she looks at it; then grows in dimension as if the
tablecloth itself were apprehending space, taking on volume,
modifying complex visual sensations.

Meanwhile, because he wants to proceed to the main course,
Mr Ramsay is annoyed when Augustus Carmichael asks for a
second helping of soup. Furthermore, the children notice their
father's irritation and are about to burst into open laughter. Mrs
Ramsay, intuitive and sagacious, knows how to commandeer her
family's attention: "Light the candles."[8] It is time to prepare for
the heart of the ritual - the *agape* or communal meal - to unite the
fragmentary, if only for a moment, in eternity.

Eight lit candles are placed on the table, where they seem to
take on the upright configuration of a church spire: "the flames
stood upright and drew with them into visibility the long table
entire."[9] Symbolically, the number eight represents eternity,
enlightenment, circularity, fluidity. What is almost an epiphany
seems to take place:

> ... and the faces on both sides of the table were brought
> nearer by the candlelight, and composed, as they had not
> been in the twilight, into a party round a table, for the
> night was now shut off by panes of glass, which, far from
> giving any accurate view of the outside world, rippled it
> so strangely that here, inside the room, seemed to be

order and dry land; there, outside, a reflection in which
things wavered and vanished, waterily.[10]

The focus here is on domestic detail: candles, plates, salt-cellar,
each of which occupies its own particular space and has its own
density and mass. The most arresting object, "a yellow and purple
dish of fruit," is in the middle of the table, the whole scene
presenting symphonic modulations in colour that range from the
ineffable gold brilliance of candle flame to blackness. The
glimmering, almost unearthly flickerings from the candles
illuminate Mrs. Ramsay's face, thereby enhancing for the reader
her archetypal nature.

The communion: The offering begins as the "Boeuf en Daube"
is now brought in and placed before Mrs Ramsay, who proceeds to
put some of the delicious stew, cooked to perfection, on each
"staring white" Plate (Host):

> And she peered into the dish, with its shiny walls and its
> confusion of savoury brown and yellow meats and its
> bay leaves and its wine and thought. This will celebrate
> the occasion - a curious sense rising in her, at once
> freakish and tender, of celebrating a festival, as if two
> emotions were called up in her, one profound - for what
> could be more serious than the love of man for woman,
> what more commanding more impressive, bearing in
> its bosom the seeds of death...[11]

Bored moments earlier, Mr Bankes now pronounces the
"Boeuf en Daube" a triumph. He puts his knife down:

> He had eaten attentively. It was rich; it was tender. It
> was perfectly cooked. How did she manage these things
> in the depths of the country? he asked her. She was a
> wonderful woman. All his love, his reverence, had
> returned; and she knew it.
> "It is a French recipe of my grandmother's," said
> Mrs. Ramsay speaking with a ring of great pleasure in
> her voice. Of course it was French. What passes for
> cookery in England is an abomination (they agreed). It
> is puttting cabbages in water. It is roasting meat till it is
> like leather. It is cutting off the delicious skins of
> vegetables.[12]

Symbolically, the meat represents the blood of deity; it is
energy - the food of life. Before the meat ceremony nothing seems
to have truly taken on life or texture; the world was barren, the

participants alienated. The succulent meat dish arouses feeling and passion; it is a hierophany possessed of its own power and magnetism, its own spiritual fermentation. Consequently, Lily finds it absurd when the sublime Mrs Ramsay begins to talk about vegetable skins. The conversation does not fit in with Lily's view of Mrs Ramsay. Yet she soon reverts to her veneration of her "irresistible" older friend, who spells "abundance" in contrast to Lily's "poverty of spirit."[13] Whenever Lily feels herself uncomfortable or overwhelmed, as if Mrs Ramsay were leading her "victims ... to the altar", she returns to her painting, considering the salt-cellar, the pattern on the tablecloth, the tree. In much the same way that Cézanne searched to discover the proper place for volume and mass in an empty picture space, so Lily pursues her quest. She also resolves not to marry; why dilute her aim?

Mrs Ramsay feels inadequate when she tries to enter the men's discussion about mathematics and other subjects - "this admirable fabric of the masculine intelligence."[14] Borrowing thoughts that are not her own confuses her; she feels lost in detail and "fire encircled." She is "forced to veil her crest, dismount her batteries."[15] This happens to those whose thinking function is underdeveloped. But Mrs Ramsay, endowed with magical understanding, offsets what might have proved her undoing by concentrating attention on the dish of fruit in the middle of the table:

> Her eyes had been going in and out among the curves
> and shadows of the fruit, among the rich purples of the
> lowland grapes, then over the horny ridge of the shell,
> putting a yellow against a purple, curved shape against
> a round shape, without knowing why she did it, or why,
> every time she did it, she felt more and more serene;
> until, oh, what a pity that they should do it - a hand
> reached out, took a pear, and spoilt the whole thing.[16]

The description of the fruit dish, a verbal Cézanne still-life, is the finale of the *agape*. Unconsciously, Mrs Ramsay keeps a jealous guard over it, for with the disappearance of the fruit comes her dethronement and fall to earth.

The beautiful centrepiece of fruit may be looked upon as a microcosm - a painting. The exquisite nature of these inanimate offerings, which Mrs. Ramsay's daughter Rose has arranged with such care, taking into account gradations in their colour and form, represent to her mother a fusion of mind and senses, a journey into the depths of her aesthetic, spiritual, and psychological being. Harmony and balance emerge from this: hence, the centrepiece of fruit is in a sense symbolic of Mrs Ramsay's life experience.

This description of the fruit dish may well be the apogee of Woolf's art. Roger Fry, the art critic, pointed out that Cézanne's still-lifes "frequently catch the purest self-revelation of the artist", and this is also true of Woolf's pictorial imagery.[17] Although the deep pure yellows and rich purple tones of the pears, bananas, and grapes in the fruit-bowl provide a synthetic summing up of Mrs Ramsay's own needs, desires, and loving nature, it is in the contemplation of the shapes of the fruit itself that a concentration of emotion takes place; a silent drama is lived out in what appears to have been a fairly eventless existence. With minute but deft touches of verbal brushstrokes, Woolf was able to re-create the psychic tension and the successive layers of a searching soul. The spirit of unity that Mrs Ramsay achieved by this lighting of the candles, the "Boeuf en Daube," and her contemplation of the dish of fruit is the goal Lily seeks to replicate - "the harmonic principle" that Lily longs to integrate in her painting.

The return: Once the meal has ended, however, the unity achieved in the Communion meal breaks up. Each person returns to his own dimension and energy pattern; the mysterious earlier agitations at the dinner table no longer crisscross in complex relational systems. Family and friends leave for other parts of the house, and the dining-room becomes empty; its shape, lustre, and patina change. Mrs Ramsay alone realises that she has undergone a numinous experience and that "nothing on earth can equal this happiness" - that is, to have a love-filled and love-bestowing existence.[18]

The "dinner" sequence is a paradigm of Woolf's mastery of the techniques of the impressionists and Cézanne in cutting through mass, dividing solids, stilling flux, and integrating fragmentary glances, thoughts, phrases, and objects into a cohesive whole by means of her indelibly arresting verbal brushstrokes. In *To the Lighthouse* Woolf created - to use Cézanne's phrase - "a union of the universe and the individual."[19]

Bettina L. Knapp

NOTES

[1] Virginia Woolf, *To the Lighthouse*, New York: Harcourt Brace, 1927, p.124.
[2] Ibid., p.125.
[3] Ibid., p.126.
[4] Ibid., p.128.
[5] Ibid., p.129.
[6] Ibid., p.130.
[7] Ibid., p.137.
[8] Ibid., p.145.
[9] Ibid., p.146.
[10] Ibid.
[11] Ibid., p.151
[12] Ibid., p.151-2
[13] Ibid., p. 152.
[14] Ibid., p. 159.
[15] Ibid., p. 156.
[16] Ibid., p. 163.
[17] Roger Fry, *Cézanne: A Study of His Development*, London: Macmillan Co., 1927, p. 4.
[18] *To the Lighthouse* , p. 186.
[19] Herschel B. Chipp, *Theories of Modern Art*, Los Angeles: University of California Press, 1973, p. 21.

4.

EATING OUT: WITH BARTHES

In his reflections on photography, *La Chambre claire*, published in 1980, Roland Barthes inscribes his homage to Jean-Paul Sartre, the Sartre of *L'Imaginaire*. The temptation to view Sartre as rival and opposite to the semiological Barthes has had its currency. Under the tutelage of André Gide, Carlyle's *Sartor Resartus*, reflected in the mirror eye of *Les Faux-Monnayeurs* ("Les idées de change, de dévalorisation, d'inflation, peu à peu envahissaient son livre, comme les théories du vêtement le *Sartor Resartus* de Carlyle - où elles usurpaient la place des personnages."),[1] became a model and inspiration for Barthes's *Système de la mode*. The culinary dimensions of Barthes's writings, an important but little noted aspect of his enterprise, parallel his musings on clothes. Le "plaisir de la table" and *Le Plaisir du texte* are conjoined. The origin is in Barthes's "fig-piece", his pastiche of Plato's account of the death of Socrates, his earliest writing, his "premier texte", "En Marge du *Criton*" published in *L'Arc* in 1974; and, I suggest, Sartre's own search for existential meaning in his food notes in *L'Etre et le Néant* relates to Barthes's interest in the apparently unreadable signs of his semiotic game and his notion of "biographèmes". Sartre's irritating throwaway lines that gave rise to my culinary reflections begun in 1972 were sandy particles relating to oysters: "Il n'est donc nullement indifférent d'aimer les huîtres ou les palourdes, les escargots ou les crevettes, pour peu que nous sachions démêler la signification existentielle de ces nourritures".[2] Barthes, too, drops a hint concerning the importance of the culinary in his interpretation of Sade and states flatly that all novels could be classified according to the frankness of their alimentary allusions: "Avec Proust, Zola, Flaubert, on sait toujours ce que mangent les personnages; avec Fromentin, Laclos ou même Stendhal, non. Le détail alimentaire excède la signification, il est le supplément énigmatique du sens (de l'idéologie)".[3]

Both Sartre and Barthes left behind them projects unfinished, incomplete, that are invitations to extend and expand their culinary, their alimentary, pleasure. In his *Barthes par Barthes*, Roland speaks of the ethnological temptation of interpretation of the most natural of objects: faces, food, clothing, and complexion, but that temptation is the temptation of the writer. One of his future, but unwritten books, was to have been "Une Encyclopédie de la Nourriture (diététique, histoire, économie, géographie, et surtout *symbolique*".[4] A second was a *Vie des hommes illustres* in which the search for "biographèmes" was the suggested *modus operandi*. A third was a book on homosexual discourse; another, a journal (diary) of desire; another on the amateur (the amator); and finally the book of life that joins the transcription of *Incidents*, those mini-texts, jottings, notations, pleats and folds of sense and sensual play. Frankness (in French *la franchise*) of culinary expression enlightens the sexual and the alimentary. It is a key to lived liberation and the new franchise that marks the "cuisse de grenouille" recipes of their kitchen art.

Barthes's invitation to dine, to eat out, is, like Sartre's, a coy, covert flirtation with the culinary and sexual partner. The detailing function of the alimentary writer is for both Sartre and Barthes the introduction of pleasure and the enigma of the links between travel, eating out, desire, and transgression in the libertine world of the freed man. Sartre's *Visages, précédé de Portraits officiels* and his *Nourritures, suivi des extraits de la Nausée* were written in the thirties; Barthes's parallel texts of the early forties are first, "En Marge du *Criton*", in which his Socrates chooses not hemlock but the sensual fig, and second, "Notes sur André Gide et son *Journal*", where the focus is not on "extracts of nausea" but on scraps ("déchets") daily collected in a journal/diary. In his novel *Barthes par Barthes*, he insists that: "Tout ceci doit être considéré comme dit par un personnage de roman".[5] He notes the disrepute into which the autobiographical journal has fallen and reminds us that in the sixteenth century "où l'on commençait à en écrire, sans répugnance, on appelait ça un diaire: diarrhée et glaire".[6] In other places I have served up some concoctions based on Sartre's *hors d'oeuvres*: "Visages et nourritures" in *Etudes Sartriennes*, "Just Desserts" in *Yale French Studies*, "Homo/textuality: Eating the Other" in *Homosexualities and French Literature*. Now I would like to propose not a fruit compote or a Neapolitan pastry but "Fig mõusse à l'Arcimboldo" sometimes called "Barthes's Fig Trifle".

The ingredients are not Sartre's snails, oysters, and shrimp but Barthes's own glair - his egg whites - and his figs blended in his cuisinart following his own diary receipt and diarrhea. The end result follows his experiment in writing out his body: "Productions de mes fragments. Contemplation de mes fragments (correction, polissage, etc.). Contemplation de mes déchets (narcissisme)".[7] The "biographèmes" are a question of taste, and if he has acquired a taste for them in writing of Sade, Fourier, and Loyola, he invites us to do the same for him:

> Si j'étais écrivain, et mort, comme j'aimerais que ma vie se réduisît, par les soins d'un biographe amical et désinvolte, à quelques détails, à quelques goûts, à quelques inflexions, disons des "biographèmes", dont la distinction et la mobilité pourraient voyager hors de tout destin et venir toucher, à la façon des atomes épicuriens, quelque corps futur, promis à la même dispersion.[8]

His fascination with Sadien chocolate, with the copious luxury of the meals of victims, with coprophagous alimentation, and the summary function of food in the Sadien city in terms of restoration, poison, fattening up, and evacuation is clearly the opposite of his own. His "biographèmes" are more akin to his sympathy for those of Fourier: "Ce qui me vient de la vie de Fourier, c'est son goût pour les mirlitons (petits pâtés parisiens aux aromates), sa sympathie pour les lesbiennes, sa mort parmi les pots de fleurs".[9] He refuses, too, the pilgrimages, visions, and macerations of Loyola, and opts for the dark, damp eyes that are his own fico facing death.

In Barthes's own corpus, his Epicurean transformation of Socrates into a fig eater is the genesis of his *table d'hôte*. His own selection of titbits continues to whet our appetite and varnish his own portrait with the white of glair, abandoning the yolk of egg tempura icons. A few details, a choice of tastes, are Epicurean atoms that brush the body of his present and future work with a different kind of luxury and sensuous pleasure that even now, unfinished, defies the bitter hemlock of death. Plato's *Criton* with the bitter poison of hemlock slips into the purple of figs and candied yellow citron.

In the rewritten margins of the *Criton*, the fig, "un fruit littéraire, biblique et arcadien" is the basic ingredient. The plot of the new tale is brief. Socrates, condemned to die, is visited by his students, his friends, who wish to convince him to come away with them, to journey to a place of fig trees flourishing. Beneath them they would sit on a terrace with cool benches of marble caressed by mist and sea breezes. There they would drink the milk of goats and eat olives and figs. They would listen to his teachings on things good and beautiful, savouring the "grain de sa voix" and the Epicurean senses of life. The action centres on whether or not to

eat - to eat a fig. The detailing of the crucial fig is frankly sensual
(*la franchise*). The tale begins with the arrival of a plate of figs
displayed by Leucithes: "Sur leurs flancs enflés par la maturité,
traînaient encore quelques gouttes glacées de rosée; la peau, dorée
et par endroits craquelée, laissait entrevoir les rangées de graines
rouges sur un lit de pulpe blanche".[10]   A warm smell of sugar
wafts above.   Tempted by the fig and all it holds for him, he
refuses: "A quoi bon, je n'aurai pas le temps seulement de les
digérer".[11]   The chill of death and marble are warmed by the
cheeks of his companions who refuse to sit on stools proffered.
They prefer to seat themselves around his bed on the cool stones of
the floor "pour goûter la fraîcheur des dalles".[12] Socrates listens
in silence to the voices of these men. He is most moved by the
words of Alcibiades and his vision of the modest house and its fig
tree near the threshold. A great silence ensues and is broken by
the arrival of the practical Crito. He is apprised of the efforts of the
young men and realizes what must be done. He whispers in
Leucithes's ear. In this silent communion Socrates abandons
reason:

> Cependant, au-delà de toutes ces raisons, il sentait en
> lui un obscur tiraillement qui, à lui seul, paraissait
> devoir le faire chanceler; c'était un désir qui ne
> touchait en rien l'esprit, mais plutôt le corps. Socrate ne
> pouvait le préciser plus: ce qui le sollicitait, était très
> vague mais très puissant, et le philosophe se demandait
> avec angoisse s'il allait succomber à la chair, après
> avoir résisté aux plus subtiles attaques de l'esprit.[13]

Socrates is shocked when at that moment a second plate of figs
arrives. They are a silent last assault on his virtue. Crito is the
only one to speak: "Nous ne t'influençons pas, Socrate". Tiresias
gently opens a window: "Un rayon de soleil vint caresser les figues
et découvrit dans leurs flancs d'or des échancrures sombres d'où
s'écoulait une tiédeur sucrée qui enivrait les sens."[14] Closing his
eyes, Socrates imagines he tastes figs blended with the saltier taste
of sea breezes to come, "vivant symbole de la liberté". Bathed in
this warm glow of liberty and frankness of tastes, Barthes's
Socrates abandons words. He acts: "Alors, très simplement, il
étendit la main et mangea une figue".[15] What of the other story?
What of history? Plato can take care of that.

Barthes's Socrates turns to his student-friends, turns away
from science and history, in order to embrace Corinthian figs and
drink - not goat milk - but the amazing wine of Crete. The tale is
literary, biblical, and Arcadian, he insists, but clearly the ripe

fruit dropping from the trees savoured by Barthes in his brief preface to this first text are figs of desire refused, figures of a future diary. The figs remain as essential biographeme:

> Restent les figues. Il y en avait dans le jardin familial, à Bayonne, petites, violettes, jamais assez mûres, ou toujours trop mûres; tantôt leur lait, tantôt leur pourriture me dégoûtait et je n'aimais pas ce fruit (que j'ai ensuite découvert tout autre au Maroc et récemment au restaurant Voltaire où on le sert dans de grandes soupières de crème fraîche).[16]

He slyly asks the essential question slipping out of the pages of Gide's *L'Immoraliste* and tentatively proposes an answer. He wonders why he turned the fig into a fruit of temptation, an immoral fruit, a philosophical fruit: "A moins que derrière la figue il n'y eût, tapi, le Sexe, Fica".[17]

The eating of the fig, a non-fruit housing the multitude of real fruits in its casing, is linked naturally to that other first text, "Notes sur André Gide et son *Journal*", that writing on the body of Gide's diary of dry heaves, glair, and the alternative diarrhea - essential ingredients of self-portraiture. Desire and dining come together once again: "On appelait ça un *diaire*". The seeds of the fig planted will not die. *Si le grain ne meurt* is Gide's fertile text of desire, but Barthes, in the thirties, like Gide before him, is unsure; even as he notes the temptation of the scientific in Gide, he embraces the scientific and historical as a buttress against the fig, initially refusing the link between eating and desire, between tricking the palate and tricking. The ethnologist, the scientist, competes with the novelist, the writer. Gide's detour to the natural sciences inspires Barthes to be led down the scientific path. For Gide's biology he substitutes linguistics in his flight from the fig. Linguistics and semiology - not semiotics characterized by the *déchet*, the biographemical ort, the edible and the eaten - are the temporary cure for the immoral fruit that would provoke disorder and flux in the body and the text, resulting in novels and narcissistic diarrhea.

The remedy is written up in *Les Annales* of 1961. "Scientific" discourse covers the invitation to eat, to dine out, to come out in full fig. Rhetoric, as in Barthes's delicious book on *Arcimboldo* (Parma and Milan: Franco Maria Ricci, 1978), hides the sensual fig. In the *Annales* article, "Pour une psycho-sociologie de l'alimentation contemporaine", the sensual is reduced to the scientific; an ambivalence that continues even in his unwritten

"Encyclopédie de la Nourriture (diététique, histoire, économie, géographie, et surtout symbolique)". The eating out, the fig dessert, the trifle, the mousse, the book on homosexual discourse are all deferred as he focuses on the sociology of the snack and the business lunch. In this article of alimentary psycho-sociology, Barthes's voice is projected semiologically - not semiotically. The multiple fruits are covered by commercial packaging and presented scientifically. Diarrhea is checked temporarily. But after these "scientific" temptations, he begins to scatter the seeds of the fig rediscovered. In his texts on Sade, Fourier, Loyola, and in his oriental excursion (*L'Empire des signes*), he toys with new food. He discovers "la virginité de sa cuisson" and abandons the procreativity of discourse with a central intention. Two things then: "aucun plat japonais n'est pourvu d'un *centre*" and the pleasure and contemplation of the fragment:

> ... la nourriture n'est jamais qu'une collection de fragments, dont aucun n'apparaît privilégié par un ordre d'ingestion: manger n'est pas respecter un menu (un itinéraire de plats), mais prélever, d'une touche légère de la baguette, tantôt une couleur, tantôt une autre, au gré d'une sorte d'inspiration qui apparaît dans sa lenteur comme l'accompagnement détaché, indirect, de la conversation (qui peut être, elle-même, fort silencieuse).[18]

Here there is no talk, only the sensual silence of the fig-eating of that first text. He plays with *baguettes* and *braguettes*, indulging his taste for the rare offerings of foreign fare. His Japan ("un pays de bonheur érotique", he confides to Renaud Camus in *Notes Achriennes*) displaces Gide's Algeria; this travel, these trips, these dining excursions, renew the old silent taste for culinary *franchise* remarked in rewritten Plato and Gide re-penned.

His fruitfulness now takes the form of recovered fragments that return us endlessly to the rewriting of history and story, a return to the journal fragment, the scrap, the ort. He embraces the other Gide in a turn to the frankly autobiographical. He reinscribes on the bed of the imaginary an insistence on what is at stake in Gide's gamble of breaking free from the scientific as fictional ground:

> J'ai l'illusion de croire qu'en brisant mon discours, je cesse de discourir imaginairement sur moi-même, j'atténue le risque de transcendance; mais comme le fragment, cette couche de langage (les déchets du narcissisme) s'offre le mieux à l'interprétation, en

croyant *me disperser*, je ne fais que regagner le lit de
l'imaginaire .[19]

Opting for warmer climes, students, friends of Socrates, and the
head cook will leave Science and Philosophy behind. Barthes's
writing changes. Silent acts of fig eating and sensuousness are
folded into the glair; the recipe is renewed and passed on from
Chef to apprentice cook. Procreation, Barthes insists in his
introduction to the *Physiologie du goût*, is a science. We know its
receipts are published in *Les Annales* where the dietetics of history
stand in for the unhealthy texts of desire. But now in Barthes's
return to the imagination, the seminal fig, the seeds burst from its
casing and are dispersed in novel texts where they are mixed with
egg whites to become grains that do not die, but are blended into a
mösusse recalling the salty air of sea froth and fico liberation.

In his preface to Brillat-Savarin's *Physiologie du goût*,
Barthes addresses the perversion of eating to nourish the body and
turns instead away from health and procreation to the *pleasure de
la table*, and the useless luxury of desire. This is a shared appetite
(the "*a*" *petit* of Voltaire couched in his response to the princely $\frac{p}{a}$ [à
souper]); accepting the invitation to sup, to dine, to eat out in letters
is a sensual, fragmented response. Like Voltaire, now of the
restaurant Voltaire where Barthes rediscovers figs in a great soup
plate covered with cream, Roland can only reply with *belles lettres*:
$\frac{G}{a}$ - "J'ai grand appétit". Those visible letters become the pleasure
of the text, the pleasure of the table, a menu read under a fig tree
in silence.

Barthes looks back. He reproaches himself, Gide, and
Brillat-Savarin for the temptation of scientific discourse.
Physiology and taste are unproductively coupled. The naïve need
no longer bracket his gifts with scientific, statistical readings.
Brillat-Savarin is like "un écrivain qui mettrait des guillemets
autour des vérités qu'il énonce, non par prudence scientifique,
mais par crainte de donner l'image d'un naïf (ce en quoi l'on peut
voir que l'ironie est toujours timide)".[20] The naïve, natural taste
for sensuous figs first inscribed in a text rewritten is uncovered in
Gide's desiring texts. Roland Barthes's old taste is resituated
through his supper in the restaurant Voltaire. The restorative
function is a mind displaced by the young body as amber figs are
supped in cream. Brillat-Savarin, a new Socrates, is the *chef*
whose gifts are warmly received:

Il lui faut mettre en scène, si l'on peut dire le *luxe* du
désir, amoureux ou gastronomique; supplément
énigmatique, inutile, la nourriture désirée - celle que
décrit Brillat-Savarin - est une perte inconditionnelle,
une sorte de cérémonie ethnographique par laquelle
l'homme célèbre son pouvoir, sa liberté de brûler son
énergie pour 'rien'.[21]

The luxury of desire has now become the co-incidence of the
amorous and the gastronomical pleasure inscribed in new recipes
for unscientific texts. *Juvenalia* is not mere child's play. *L a
cuisine n'est pas un jeu d'enfants.*

George Bauer

NOTES

[1] André Gide, *Romans, Récits et Soties*, Paris: Gallimard, 1958, p. 1085. "The
ideas of change, of devaluation, of inflation, little by little invaded his book, like
the theories of clothes Carlyle's *Sartor Resartus*, where they usurped the place of
the characters." (The translations are my own in each case.)

[2] Jean-Paul Sartre, *L'Etre et le Néant*, Paris: Gallimard, 1943, p. 707. "It is in
no way a matter of indifference to like oysters or clams, snails or shrimp, if
only we know how to unravel the existential meaning of these foods."

[3] Roland Barthes, *Sade, Fourier, Loyola*, Paris: Seuil, 1971, p. 129. "With
Proust, Zola, Flaubert, you always know what the characters eat; with
Fromentin, Laclos, or even Stendhal, no. The alirentary detail is in excess of
signification, it is the enigmatic supplement of meaning (of ideology)."

[4] Roland Barthes, *Barthes par Barthes*, Paris: Seuil, 1975, p. 153. "All of this
must be considered as if said by a character in a novel."

[5] Ibid. (inside front cover).

[6] Ibid., p. 99. "when they began to write them, without repugnance, they called it
a *diaire*: diarrhea and glair."

[7] Ibid. "Production of my fragments. Contemplation of fragments (correcting,
polishing, etc.). Contemplation of my offal (narcissism)."

[8] *Sade, Fourier, Loyola*, p. 14. "If I were a writer, and dead, how I would love to
have my life, through the care of a friendly, unconstrained biographer, reduced
to a few details, a few tastes, a few inflections, to what we will call
'biographemes', whose distinction and mobility might travel outside of any fate

and come to touch, like Epicurean atoms, some future body, promised the same dispersion."

[9] Ibid. "What comes to me from Fourier's life is his taste for *mirlitons* (Parisian spice cakes), his sympathy for lesbians, his death among the flowerpots."

[10] Roland Barthes, "En marge du *Criton*", *L'Arc*, no. 56, p. 4. "On their sides swollen with ripeness, a few drops of glistening dew lingered; the golden skin was crackled in places revealing the rows of red seeds on a bed of white pulp."

[11] Ibid. "To what good, I will not even have the time to digest them."

[12] Ibid. "in order to taste the freshness of the *dalles*".

[13] Ibid., p. 6. "Nevertheless, beyond all these reasons, he felt in him an obscure gnawing that, to him alone, seemed to make him waver; it was a desire that had nothing to do with the mind, but rather the body. Socrates was unable to be more precise: what was tempting him was very vague, but very powerful. The philosopher asked himself in anguish if he was going to give into the flesh after having resisted the most subtle attacks on the mind."

[14] Ibid., p. 7. "We are not influencing you, Socrates." "A ray of sunshine came to caress the figs and revealed on their golden flesh dark indentations out of which flowed a sugary warmth that intoxicated the senses."

[15] Ibid. "Then, quite simply, he reached out his hand and ate a fig."

[16] Ibid., p. 4. "Still, the figs. There were some in the family garden in Bayonne: small, violet/purple, never ripe enough or always too ripe; sometimes the fig-milk, sometimes the rottenness, disgusted me and I never cared for this fruit (I have since discovered them very different in Morocco and recently in the Restaurant Voltaire where they are served in large soup plates of *crème fraîche*)."

[17] Ibid. "Unless behind the fig there was lurking, *le Sexe*, Fica?"

[18] Roland Barthes, *L'Empire des signes*, Geneva: Skira, 1980, pp. 33-34. "No Japanese dish has a *centre*." "The fare is never anything but a collection of fragments in which none of the fragments are privileged by a sequence of ingesting: eating is not respecting the menu (an itinerary of dishes) but a sampling, with a slight touch of the chopstick, one colour, then another, a whimsical kind of inspiration that in its slow movement appears as a detached, indirect accompaniment for the conversation (which itself can be very quiet)."

[19] *Barthes par Barthes*, p. 99. "I have the illusion of believing that in interrupting my discourse, ceasing to discourse imaginarily on myself, I decrease the risk of transcendence; but like the fragment, that couch of language (the offal of narcissism) best lends itself to interpretation, in believing *my dispersion*, I only regain the bed of the imaginary." The emphasis is mine.

[20] Roland Barthes, "Lecture de Brillat-Savarin", in *Physiologie du goût* by Brillat-Savarin, Paris: Hermann, 1975, p. 28. "a writer who would put quotation marks around the verities he puts forth, not out of scientific prudence, but for fear of giving the appearance of being naïve (in this, one can see that irony is always timid)."

[21] Ibid., p. 9. "He must bring on stage, if it can be named, the *luxury* of desire, amorous or gastronomical; enigmatic supplement, useless, the fare desired -

that described by Brillat-Savarin - is an unconditional loss, a kind of ethnographic ceremony through which man celebrates his power, his freedom to burn his energy for 'nothing'."

5.

INTRODUCING *THE CANLIT FOODBOOK*[1]

I'm one of those people who read cookbooks the way other people read travel writing: I may not ever make the recipe, but it's fun to read about it, and to speculate on what kind of people would. One man's cookbook is another woman's soft porn; there's a certain sybaritic voyeurism involved, an indulgence by proxy. But it's informative too: you know other countries partly through their typical foods, so why not your own? Any cookbook, read in its entirety, creates its own imagined view of its world: so *that's* what they had for breakfast! I think I first connected literature with eating when I was twelve and reading *Ivanhoe*: there was Rebecca, shut up romantically in a tower, but what did she have to eat?

It seemed logical, then, to investigate the eating aberrations of Canadians through their literature, and to examine the literature itself with an eye to the consuming passions, or lack of them, described therein. I found out fairly quickly that authors could be divided into two groups: those that mention food, indeed revel in it, and those that never give it a second thought. Some novelists make sure that their characters are given a square meal, or at least a disgusting one, at rapid intervals; others merely furnish them with drink; others neglect their digestive tracts entirely. Some poets ask nothing more than a lemon, pear or grape to set off their meditative processes, others confine themselves to dead skunks and automobile parts. So if your favourite writers are not in here, there may be a simple reason for it.

The CanLit Foodbook is not exactly a cookbook; on the other hand, it isn't exactly not a cookbook, either. Viewed one way, it's a civilized literary symposium on the subject of food, containing, as it does, a great many extracts selected from Canadian poetry and prose, past, present, and coast-to-coast, on the subject of some of the things people put into their mouths with a view to ingestion. Viewed another way, it's a collection of recipes preceded by some amusing verbal shenanigans. In addition, it's a shameless fundraiser: I put it together in aid of the P.E.N. International Writers In Prison Programme and the Writers' Development Trust, stupidly thinking that this approach would be easier than pestering writers until they disgorged their favourite recipes. As it turns out, I did this also, and the project took three times as much time as it would have if I'd stuck to simple pestering. A word here about writers, their writing and their cookery: the relation between word and deed is not so simple as you think. That is, some write about it but don't do it, others do it but don't write about it, some do both, and others do neither. Sort of like sex.

"You are what you eat" means one thing to a nutritionist, another to a novelist. Standard cookbooks put various foods in because they taste good, are easy or interesting to cook, or are good for you; authors put them in because they reveal character, slimy as well as delectable, or provide metaphors or jumping-off points into the ineffable or the inferno. It's not surprising, then, that some of the foods described here are not anything you'd want to actually eat, and some are there to deliberately provoke revulsion. A lot can be conveyed, too, about one ethnic group's views of another by the way they react to each other's treasured foodstuffs: as more than one author reminds us, one man's sea-squirt is another's *hors-d'oeuvre*.

Cultures as well as individuals tend to arrange the potentially edible into various standard divisions. Lowest on the totem pole come things that may look like food but are actively poisonous, such as *amanita muscaria* mushrooms and deadly nightshade berries. Next come things which might potentially be eaten but are considered disgusting: earthworms and slugs fall into that category for us, though others gobble them up with no problem. Next come foods that are known to be foodstuffs for some, but which are taboo to others for religious reasons: meat for Sikhs and pigs for Orthodox Jews, for instance. The taboo of taboos for most of us is human flesh, nutritious as it doubtless is; but more of that later.

Next comes our ordinary diet: those things that are so familiar to us we eat them with barely a second thought, though a skilful novelist can make us have second thoughts even about these. Next come exotic delicacies, "company food": harder to get, more expensive or harder to prepare, and therefore valued. When writers are dealing with social pretensions, a few of these are likely to be tabled. Next come foods for festive occasions: we don't have these every day, we save them for special times, and they help us mark our seasons. And finally there are sacramental foods, the eating of which is a celebration of our unity with each other and with the divine principle in our universe. Almost all religions observe the custom of offering food and saying thanks for it.

For a person whose religion is lived at a profound level, any food may be sacramental. For a starving person, much is edible that would otherwise not be. For an anorexic, on the other hand, all food may be taboo. Eating is our earliest metaphor, preceding our consciousness of gender difference, race, nationality and language. We eat before we talk.

All of which gives writers an enormous source of rich (as we say in the trade) material to work with, and work with it they have. I've arranged the chapters in this book according to the goodies that came to hand, and in what seemed to me a logical and easy-to-follow progression (though one woman's logic is another's chocolate-covered grasshopper).

We begin with a Preprandial Prologue, a series of passages that, taken together, give us a sampling of the entire range of response to and speculation about the act of eating - from the ecstatic to the repulsive, from Where Does It Come From to Where Does It Go. Poets excel here, given as they are to metaphoric pyrotechnics.

We continue with Breakfast. The bulk of the breakfast food I collected was in fact by poets - breakfast seems to do something for poets that lunch does not do. It may be the eggs. In any case, I tried for a range of breakfasts past and present, realistic and symbolic. Help yourselves. In the recipe section of this chapter, however, I tried to dish out a few things the writers themselves do not; otherwise it would have been bacon and eggs and coffee *ad redundum*.

For some reason, nobody seems to write much about lunch. I don't know the reason for this. Perhaps it's too late in the day for poets and not late enough for novelists, and business lunches have not yet impacted, as they say, on literature. In any case I couldn't gather enough lunches for a full chapter. On the other hand, there were enough fruit and vegetable poems to fill many a crate. Novelists don't usually take time out to rhapsodize on the beauties and intricacies of the common apple or garden onion, but for poets such verbal acts of worship are almost *de rigueur*. It's noteworthy that round or oblong fruits and vegetables inspire much more verse than do knobbly or frilly ones; the mandala shape, perhaps? There aren't many poems written about cauliflowers or Brussels sprouts, for instance. Recipes for this section were a slight problem, since most of the poems in question presented their subjects uncooked, and what sort of a recipe is "peel and place on a plate"? However, I cheated and put in recipes involving the application of heat. I did not include the recipe for Al Purdy's Wild Grape Wine, however. It's been known to frighten a lot of people, since it comes out about the same colour as it goes in.

If lunches were notably absent from the material examined, teas were ominously present. This may be the bit that separates the Canucks from the Yanks: Canadians, in prose as well as verse, from coast to coast, still write about Tea. For some reason I do not fathom, Tea is presented as, on the whole, a somewhat sinister occasion. Things go wrong at it, innuendoes of a shadowy kind take place, all is not well. I picked up a new novel - Tom Marshall's *Adele at the End of the Day* - the other day, and lo and behold, there was another unpleasant teatime episode, an old lady threatened with forced exorcism by two unsavoury cult members who were gorging themselves in advance from a well-laden tea-tray. Sociologists, what do you have to say about this?

In Chapter Five, the rapt mood of the poets face to face with an orange gives way to queasiness and guilt when it comes to animal protein. Most of them know perfectly well where such things as wings and breasts come from, though the rest of us may forget mid-meal. Prose writers are not so squeamish. I have to say here that Canadian literature, coast to coast, is literally squirming with fish. I could have done a whole anthology of fish stories alone. Seems they're as important in the minds of the writers as they are in those of government negotiators, a rare overlap.

The next chapter, "The Exploding Supper", is mostly prose - for in the evening the novelists come into their own. What better occasion than supper to get hostile members of a family together, stage a domestic tiff or romantic *tête-à-tête*? There's everything in this chapter, from tooth soup to nut cases. Most of the food described is fairly awful, but there's nothing a novelist revels in more than a bad dinner.

In the seventh chapter we discover what we already knew: Canadians have a sweet tooth. This is the province of the doughnut, the cake, the pudding and the pie, and even the poets can't make any of this sound too disgusting. There are some variations, too, on the theme of bread, which has other and more profound cultural and verbal resonances than, say, "sticky bun". The recipes include some wonderful fattening yummies.

In Chapter Eight, "Quaint and Curious Dishes", I've put things you might have second thoughts about eating straight off the bat. One starving explorer's rat may be another northern scientist's wolf-diet experiment and yet another Toronto poet's nasty threat, but in no case does the thought inspire gustatorial relish. For this reason, and for another one - who wants to be responsible for food poisoning? - I haven't tried any recipes here. Also the problem of how to get a rat jellied, into the fridge, but still alive and steaming, defeated me.

Chapter Nine is devoted to cannibalism, metaphorical and actual, of which there's a surprising amount in Canadian Literature. It appears to be one of those thrill-of-the-forbidden literary motifs, like the murders in murder mysteries, that we delight to contemplate, though we would probably not do it for fun, except in children's literature, where devouring and being devoured appears to be a matter of course. Which hooks in with an observable fact: kids like to eat anthropomorphic food. Who knows why? Some permissible form of naughtiness, or merely a wish to be friendly with your food? In any case, our recipes here are slanted towards the young at heart, the Frankensteins *manqué*, and the food sculptors among us.

Chapter Ten is called "Shindigs", and ends the book with a bash or two. It's devoted to scenes in which the novelists pull out all the stops, on a large scale. What better than a crowded social gathering to show us at our worst? Cocktail parties spread social snobbery before us in all its dingy feathers; weddings are great for orgies of consumption and for getting people into the same room who would ordinarily not speak to one another; Christmas dinners are unmatched for spectacles of gorging and as paradigms of moral collapse. Some of our Shindigs are realistic depictions, others flights of fancy, but all are fun. Even the funerals are strangely euphoric; and the final piece is a lovely resurrection scene, complete with a simple, sacramental Mennonite potato salad, thus returning us to the metaphysical plane from which we started out.

By the time you get to the end, you may have discovered some new recipes you want to try. But even if not, you'll certainly have encountered some new ways of looking at food. Deconstructing your dinner, as the postmodernists would have it. Food, as they used to say, for thought. Alphabet Soup.

Enjoy.

Margaret Atwood

NOTE

1 Originally written on behalf of the Writers' Development Trust of Canada.

6.

THE SUCCULENT GENDER: EAT HER SOFTLY

> She's as good, very near,
> As a ripe melting peach in September.
> ...
> She's like a rich dish
> Of venison or fish,
> That cries from the table, come eat me!
> (Unknown)

From time immemorial the female has been identified with edible commodities. For the Elizabethans it was almost cliché to compare her complexion with whipped cream, her cheeks with ripening peaches and her lips with red cherries. Similarly, the Middle-East has identified her with a veritable banquet of exotic delights: her cheeks are pomegranates; her lips luscious grapes; her breasts apples smoothed with myrrh; her navel an oasis, where camels and, perchance, men love to drink; her stomach a sheaf of corn and her pubic hair an orchard inlaid with an alabaster fountain. As we move to Africa, the female is transmuted into a tropical menu. Inevitably, her apple-like breasts are metamorphosed into fibrous plantains, while her stomach is transmuted into a watermelon. "A woman", after all "is a cob of corn into which men love to sink their teeth", so says one African whose appetite is, regrettably, larger than his good sense. It seems that when the female hits his stomach, she hits his most insatiable spot. The question remains: by what perverse irony did woman, the fructifier of the earth, degenerate into an edible commodity for the consumption and satisfaction of the male palate?

Is it possible that, undressed and in the raw, the female satisfies a primitive lust for food? For the libelous and scatological Restoration poets, she was just that. In an erotic-cum-gastronomical duet between man and woman, the man pugnaciously ventures to bury his teeth in woman's flesh:

> Woman: "Hold, hold, sir, you strike me sore. Will you
>   murder the vanquished, and never give o'er?"
> Man: "No," (cannibal-like) "on thy flesh I will feed.
>   'Tis not mercy to pity, though thou doest bleed."[1]

Does woman relish this primitive passion? Without a shadow of doubt, claims her rakish interpreter:

> Her legs were girt about my waist,
> My hands under her crupper.
> And who should say, "Now break your fast,
> And come again to supper?"[2]

Does he break his fast? Consider the repast:

> Her cherry lip, moist, plump and fair,
> Millions of kisses crown,
> Which ripe and uncropt dangled there,
> And weigh the branches down.
>
> Her breasts that swelled so plump and high
> Bred pleasant pain in me.
> For all the world I do defy
> The like felicity.
> Her thighs and belly, soft and fair,
> To me were only shown.
> To have seen such meat, and not to have eat,
> Would have angered any stone.[3]

Must she be consumed? Decidedly, attests an anonymous scrivener, especially her maidenhead, which is apt to shrivel and mould with time, providing food, needless to say, for Marvell's worms:

> Clothes that embroider'd be with gold,
> If never worn, will quickly mold.
> If in time you do not pluck
> The damasyn [plum] or the apricocke,
> In pinching Autumn they'll be dead.
> Then lose in time thy maidenhead.[4]

This ribald frankness is characteristic of the Restoration wits. Indisputably, the sexual mores were loose. Prostitution was rampant. Whores plied their trade openly, "feeding" men's fantasies while ignoring the raised eyebrows of the clergy. Resplendent in its lechery, the seventeenth century multiplied analogies between woman and food.

The eighteenth century was no better. Woman remains a delectable titbit, to touch, bite, chew and regurgitate, if sated. Unlike the Elizabethans, the eighteenth century gallants did not sing to plump lips and peach cheeks, they bit into them. A rich man in the eighteenth century could buy "the finest clothing, the noblest houses, the most costly meats and drinks and have his choice of the most beautiful females".[5] The proximity of meat and drink to females may not be coincidental, for the rich man could, simply, gorge his appetite with laced dead meat and unlaced female meat.

For Victorians the cojoining of women and food was sanctified. They glorified both woman and her kitchenette functions, making cookery as beguiling as the female herself. In cookery lay the enchantment of Circe, the mystery of Cleopatra and the witchery of Medea. The pent-up, hermetically-sealed, stove-heated dens of life immurement were transmuted in men's imaginations into lairs of potent magic, from which issued loaves and fishes.[6]

The drudgery of cookery is covered over with the same flounces, frills, lace and trimmings as were the suffocatingly uncomfortable, tightly-laced gowns of breath-holding Victorian women.

Allegedly sanctimonious, the nineteenth century had its profane streak. It continued to serve its most luscious girls to the finicky stomachs of rich men, as the following episode will testify:

> In Edwardian days an exceedingly rich man decided to test the claim of Maxim's of Paris that it would serve a customer any dish he desired, no matter how exotic. The rich gentleman ordered a naked girl covered with cherry sauce. He got her silver platter and all, in one of Maxim's private dining rooms.[7]

The acquisition of those "blank spaces of the earth", in itself an instance of territorial gluttony, gave middle-class Englishmen access to delicacies, which at one time were the monopoly of the aristocracy. By extension, the distinction between ordinary food vs. expensive food was applied to women. There were "bread-and-butter women", wholesome yet common, and "caviar" treats, expensive and stylish, as Rufus observes in "A Dangerous Woman": "Of all things in the world I detest one of those bread-and butter young girls, full of life and animal spirits".[8] Elegant women had affinities with fine whipped cream, which floated on the breasts of quivering jellies. In Elinor Wylie's *Jennifer Lorn*, Gerald, the newly-married husband, divides his time between feeding his exquisitely porcelain-like wife with a silver spoon and, subsequently, whipping up the icings with his tongue. He feeds and consumes her by turns. First, her stomach is stroked:

> For a whole week Jennifer was inconsolable; she wept continually, and grew so thin that Gerald spent many hours seated by her side, with a silver spoon in one hand and a glazed pot of Chantilly cream in the other; every time she opened her little mouth he put a spoonful of cream into it.[9]

Next, his stomach, with connecting appendages, is served:

> His eyes, however, pale, prominent, and now very lustrous in the firelight, devoured her with a curious intensity of gaze which seemed, mild and delicate as a cat's tongue, to lick up the cream of her beauty and swallow it with quiet satisfaction.[10]

Later, captive in a Middle East harem, Jennifer is cleaned, spiced, fattened, and trimmed to serve the jaded stomach of the prince, Kerim Khan:

> "She is pretty even now; when she is fat she will be prettier," said the Banou unctuously, pinching Jennifer's pointed chin. "She is not my favourite type, I confess; she has neither salt in her complexion nor spice in her mouth. But she will make a very wholesome breakfast for Kerim Khan; he is too old for highly seasoned dishes." She laughed long and horribly.[11]

The preparation of her body as a seasoned dish is no different from the "English lamb" that the prince may enjoy for breakfast:

> Do you not consider that a little English lamb, tender and toothsome, might tempt our Kerim's failing appetite? Display your genius, dear Abbas, to-night if ever; dress your lamb with sweet herbs and pistachio nuts, roast her in your silver oven; the Khan will give you half his kingdom for a slice of that delicate flesh.[12]

Now, for the wine list. The nineteenth century merchandised women for export, the same as they did wine. Not put into bottles and sold by the dozen, Harrison, the American, informs Marjoribanks, the Englishman, in "New England Women", but so that customers might select individual samples, warranted to be tonic in character, sound, of admirable bouquet, a genuine article, the pure juice of grape. The New England women, asserts Harrison, with the liquid speech of a wine merchant, should be cultivated in Johannisberge, but:

> ... the supply is necessarily limited; we cannot fill our
> orders for that, so we furnish a fine Ausleser, the first
> dropping of the grape, from our vineyards which grow
> on the bleak hillsides of Maine, New Hampshire,
> Vermont, Massachusetts, Connecticut, and Rhode
> Island. Cold winters and short summer, a great deal of
> cultivation, Puritan style of clipping the tendrils, not
> much richness of soil, not much richness any way, and
> we bring to perfection the rarest, purest, most peculiar
> grape in all the world![13]

The Englishman has reservations about the flavour of New England women. They are, perhaps, a little too pronounced, a little cold, a trifle forbidding, perhaps too intellectual, not so charming as the bottled women of New York, the south and west.

Why the ubiquity of this metaphor? The commonsensical answer is that food appeals to four of the five senses: sight, touch, taste and smell.[14] Women, when garnished, are comely to the eyes, smooth to the touch, fragrant to the nose and, with strawberry-flavoured lipstick, sensuous to the tongue. The kiss, for the anthropologist, Sir E.B. Tylor, means "a salute by taste", of the same origin as the German *küß* and the Gothic *kustus*, meaning taste.[15] The two, women and food, like Tweedledum and Tweedledee, are inseparable in people's imagination. Indeed, the two are so inextricably intermeshed that not only is woman described as food, but food as woman. Why else would an advertisement for chicken in a grocery store proclaim: "Surprise your husband with a pair of well-turned legs"?[16] Why else would the tomato blush to see the salad dressing? Dali, somewhat outlandishly, paints this point home. He has an extra-long, phallic-like French bread, ridden by two aggressive egg yolks, sodomize a small, helpless-looking Portuguese crust.[17] Finally, there is aphorism XIV of Brillat-Savarin: "A dinner which ends without cheese is like a beautiful woman with only one eye".[18]

If women and food overlap, so do copulating and eating: both involve in the words of Levi-Strauss, "une conjonction par complémentarité", the union of two separate, but complementary units.[19] In layman's terms, in eating, man, a species from one domain, unites with food, an item from a separate domain. Similarly, in copulating, man, the male gender, unites, granted some differences in taste, with a being from the female gender.

An apt example of the intimate alliance between food and copulation is described in Tennessee Williams "Gift of an Apple". A boy of nineteen approaches a huge, black-haired, squaw-like woman, in the hope of first enjoying a dinner prepared by the woman and then "having" the woman sexually. The woman hands the boy an apple. As he eats it, his imagination identifies the squirting juices of the apple with the anticipated sexual juices of the woman. Eating the apple and having the woman are cojoined activities:

> He seated himself on the bottom step, at the same time raising the apple to his mouth. The hard red skin popped open, the sweet juice squirted out and his teeth sank into the firm white meat of the apple. It is like the act of love, he thought, as he ground the skin and pulp between his jaw teeth. His tongue rolled around the front of his mouth and savored the sweet-tasting juice. He licked the outside of his lips and felt them curving into a sensuous smile. The pulp dissolved in his mouth. He tried not swallowing it. Make it last longer, he thought. But it melted like snow between his grinding teeth. It all turned to liquid and flowed on down his throat. He couldn't stop it. It is like the act of love, he thought again. You try to make it last longer. Draw out the sweet final moment. But it can't be held at that point. It has to go over and down, it has to be finished. And then you feel cheated somehow.[20]

Uninvited to dinner and bed, the boy rationalizes that the woman was probably not worth the sex act: "He could still taste the apple that he had eaten. The inside of his mouth was fresh and sweet with that taste. Maybe it was better that way, just having that taste in his mouth, the clean white taste of the apple."[21]

Other factors have contributed to the cojoining of women with food and food with copulation. It is her domain, be it the patting of pastry, the peeling of potatoes, the kneading of bread, the boiling of corn, or, *haute cuisine* of meringues, icings and glazes.

For one traditional woman, writing in 1892 for *The Householder*, her self-esteem was measured by the lightness of her biscuit batter, the tenderness of her steak and the flavour of her coffee. For another modern woman, resistant to cooking, the eternal rounds of toasting make her feel as though she is a mere appliance with a pudendum: "But Tom", says Miriam in *Small Changes*, "I might as well be any woman. I'm a warm body, I listen to you, I make breakfast. I'm a toaster with a cunt."[22]

Again, in a literal sense, woman is food because her breasts provide milk for the infant. The image of breasts for nourishment is so deeply embedded in man's psyche that it is borrowed as a metaphor to illustrate the nourishing power of God. In the eighth Ode of Solomon, God says: "My own breasts I prepared for them, that they might drink my holy milk and live thereby". Or in Peter's words, Christians are fed not by mother's milk but by "the milk of the word". This may be an unconscious urge to usurp the generative powers of the female, yet it shows the strong equation of breasts and food, spiritual as well as physical.

But to return to theoretical reasons that might explain this curious phenomenon of female edibility. A factor that may have contributed to legitimizing the gluttony of the male in consuming the female is the theory, prevalent well into the nineteenth century, that women have no core. They are matter, bereft of soul or essence, while man is mind, endowed with the highest worth of existence. As matter, woman is a composite of fleshly lusts, merely in the world to procreate, while man is a composite of idealist aspirations. Bereft of soul, she is unadulterated carnality which, like the flesh and pulp of food, can be consumed.

Otto Weininger, a reputable misogynist and dangerous derelict, waxed eloquently on the spiritual vacuum, the *nada* quality, of women:

> Women have no existence and no essence; they are not, they are nothing. Mankind occurs as male or female, as something or nothing. Woman has no share in ontological reality, no relation to the thing-in-itself, which, in the deepest interpretation, is the absolute, is God. Man in his highest form, the genius, has such a relation, and for him the absolute is either the conception of the highest worth of existence, in which case he is a philosopher; or it is the wonderful fairyland of dreams, the kingdom of absolute beauty, and then he is an artist. But both views mean the same. Woman has no relation to the idea, she neither affirms nor denies it; she is neither moral nor anti-moral; mathematically speaking, she has no sign; she is purposeless, neither good nor bad, neither angel nor devil, never egotistical (and therefore has often been said to be altruistic); she is

as non-moral as she is non-logical. But all existence is
moral and logical existence. So woman has no
existence.[23]

Otto Weininger would be much surprised by a current supposition
that reverses his appraisal regarding the *nada* quality of women.
In *The Fat Woman's Joke*, Esther Sussman, the obese, food-loving
heroine, declares that it is men who lack substance in women's
eyes. They are "figments of lust" and vague "sources of despair".
The least a man can do, in the circumstances, is to "endevor to
exist well truly in the flesh".[24] A woman can believe in a man who
looks solid, given his absence of qualities that relate to character.
It is the other way around with women: "A woman has all too
much substance in a man's eyes at the best of times." That is why
men like women to be slim. "Her lack of flesh negates her. The
less of her there is, the less notice he need take of her."[25] The more
like a male she appears to be, that is in her lack of substance, the
safer he feels. It would seem that since Weininger's time, women
have expanded in substance and men diminished in it, at least in
the perception of this discerning heroine.

There are other speculations. Jealousy of woman's
procreative powers may be an additional factor in promoting
metaphors of edibility. Dr Freud has informed the world of "penis
envy". Feminist psychology, in a bid to right the balance, has
introduced "vagina envy". This envy, reflected in the sinister
designs of the male to usurp the reproductive functions of the
female, once a curious idea, is now almost considered a cliché.
Zeus, in a splendid gesture of self-sufficiency, delivered Athena
fully-armed from his forehead, no doubt the first "brain child" of a
man. Myth has it that this labour of love did induce a headache,
but not strong enough to restrain the urge of increasing his brood.
Next, he thunder-clapped the foetus of Dionysius into one athletic
thigh, effected a lightning-quick sewing job on the section and,
later, with god-like ease delivered Dionysius. The Greek God was
not singular in possessing a fertile womb-brain. The Christian
God, who gave birth to Adam, is a close second, and Adam, made
in God's image, perpetuated the trick. He gave birth to Eve.

Male deliveries do not terminate with the gods. When Robert
Schumann finished composing *The Spring Symphony*, he said he
felt "like a young wife first delivered of a child - so light, so happy,
and yet so ill and weak."

In a similar vein, and curiously, entries of births in the *San Francisco Examiner* (cf. August 14, 1975) fail to mention the mother's name:

> BIRTHS
> Born to:
> ANDREWS, Norman ... [address] ... May 8, 1975, a daughter ...
> BRUBAKER, Randall ... [address] ... May 23, 1975, a son ...

There are other symptoms of womb envy. In *The Travels*, Marco Polo observed a curious habit of males in the province of Zardandan:

> These people have the following singular usage. As soon as a woman has been delivered of a child, and rising from her bed, has washed and swaddled the infant, her husband immediately takes the place she has left, has the child laid beside him, and cares for it for forty days. In the meantime, friends and relations pay him their visits of congratulation, while the woman attends to the business of the house, carries food and drink to the husband in his bed, and suckles the infant at his side.[26]

This quaint practice that ethnologists call "couvade", which consists of the father taking to his bed with the newborn child while the mother gets up and waits on him hand and food, has been noted in Africa, Borneo, India, and especially among the aborigines of North and South America.[27] This practice may be, among other things, the male attempt at simulating the birth processes of the female, which he consciously, or unconsciously, desires.

Perceiving woman as food may be an unconscious attempt on the part of men to internalize her fructifying powers. This urge may stem from remotest history. The Abipones of Paraguay eat jaguars, bulls and stags to make them strong, brave and swift. The Miris of Assam prize tigers' flesh to make themselves fierce - but forbid it to their women; the Kansas Indians relish dogs' flesh on the grounds that by eating it they become brave and faithful. These are a few of the tribal beliefs about the magic of food.[28] Is it possible that men eat women, even though metaphorically, to acquire kinship with their female powers?

Yet, all is not kosher. The Abipones of Paraguay avoid eating hens and tortoises for fear of becoming cowardly and slow. The Ainu of Japan, who believe the otter to be a forgetful animal, refuse to eat it lest by so doing they lose their memory.[29] Why, then, it may be asked, would men lust after female flesh, when women are allegedly the weaker sex and, therefore, unacceptable meat? Could it be that even though males articulate contempt for her weakness, they secretly envy the power that her procreative gifts bestow on her? Or could it be that men are ambivalent? Lust and repulsion can be bed partners. After all a meal is followed by a belch. Men eat women and belch them at their pleasure.

This insidious process of female assimilation by the male is described with sensitivity and humour in Margaret Atwood's *The Edible Woman.* The novel describes the passage of Marian's consciousness from confusion to relative clarity regarding the nature of her heterosexual relationships. The insights presented have universal significance concerning the imbalance of the sexes.

Early in the novel, Marian is aware of the unequal power ratio between Peter and herself. She is a silent and solid crutch, a two-dimensional "stage-prop" on which Peter leans. In meeting his ever-increasing emotional needs, she dwindles into a papier-maché cipher, while he expands into a fully-functioning, social being. Clara, an academically aware feminist friend, puts her finger on the spot when she dilates, at a party, on the especial problems of educated women in marriage:

> "I think it's harder for any woman who's been to university. She gets the idea she has a mind, her professors pay attention to what she has to say, they treat her like a thinking human being; when she gets married, her core gets invaded. ..."
> "Her what?" Marian asked.
> "Her core. The centre of her personality, the thing she's built up; her image of herself, if you like."
> "Oh. Yes", said Marian.
> "Her feminine role and her core are really in opposition, her feminine role demands passivity from her. ..."
> Marian had a fleeting vision of a large globular pastry, decorated with whipped cream and maraschino cherries, floating suspended in the air above Joe's head.
> "So she allows her core to get taken over by the husband. And when the kids come, she wakes up one morning and discovers she doesn't have anything left

> inside, she's hollow, she doesn't know who she is any
> more; her core has been destroyed."[30]

As the guests depart, Marian feels like a "two-dimensional small figure in a red dress, posed like a paper woman in a mail-order catalogue, turning and smiling, fluttering in the white empty space ...".[31] As she smiles at Peter, "[s]he sensed her face as vastly spreading and papery and slightly dilapidated: a huge billboard smile, peeling away in flaps and patches, the metal surface beneath showing through ...".[32]

The process of character erosion has been steady. Earlier, staring into the mirror, she wonders if she has any central core. What was it that lay beneath the surface these pieces [ear-rings, hair] were floating on, holding them all together?

> She held both of her naked arms out toward the mirror.
> They were the only portion of her flesh that was without a
> cloth or nylon or leather or varnish covering, but in the
> glass even they looked fake, like soft pinkish-white
> rubber or plastic, boneless, flexible ...[33]

Her panic at being non-existent reaches its climax when she decides to dramatize her non-personhood by baking a cake in the shape of her own person and allowing Peter to consume it. "'Sponge or angel-food?' she wondered. She decided on sponge. It was more fitting."[34] Marian operates on the cake the way Peter had operated on her:

> She scooped out part of it and made a head with the
> section she had taken out. Then she nipped in a waist at
> the sides. The other half she pulled into strips for the
> arms and legs. The spongy cake was pliable, easy to
> mould. She stuck all the separate members together with
> white icing, and used the rest of the icing to cover the
> shape she had constructed. It was bumpy in places and
> had too many crumbs in the skin, but it would do. She
> reinforced the feet and ankles with tooth-picks.[35]

She was bits and pieces of flesh and functions for him. He allowed her no integrity of personhood, having invaded her core to its centre. She was no more than shaped cake, flour, sugar, icing and colour slapped together. Her cake was how she perceived herself:

> Her creation gazed up at her, its face doll-like and
> vacant except for the small silver glitter of intelligence

in each green eye. While making it she had been
almost gleeful, but now, contemplating it, she was
pensive. All that work had gone into the lady and now
what would happen to her?
"You look delicious," she told her. "Very appetizing.
And that's what will happen to you; that's what you get
for being food."[36]

She carries the cake to Peter "with reverence, as though she
was carrying something sacred in a procession, an icon or the
crown on a cushion in a play".[37] Kneeling, she made her speech:

"You've been trying to destroy me, haven't you," she
said. "You've been trying to assimilate me. But I've
made you a substitute, something you'll like much
better. This is what you really wanted all along, isn't
it? I'll get you a fork," she added somewhat
prosaically.

Throughout history, says Una Stannard, in *Mrs Man*,
woman's lot had been to disappear from the earth as if she had
never lived. Margaret Atwood's Marian consigns herself to
oblivion by offering herself in mock ritual, as a sacrificial cake at
the altar of Peter's ego. He has annihilated her integrity in
devious ways; she now gives him the choice of slicing her throat,
spooning her breasts and munching her flanks, blatantly.

There may be a dash of "revenge cannibalism" in the male
urge to devour the female. Once again the belief structure
associated with cannibalism may clarify this idea. The eating of
human flesh represented in some cultures a way of securing
revenge on the enemy "not unlike the displaying of a victim's head
on a post or spike or the cutting up of the body, ...":[38]

It was by no means an uncommon occurrence for
outraged Tang citizenry to chop up the body of a corrupt
or tyrannical official and eat him ... In 739 an officer of
the court, who enjoyed the monarch's favor, accepted a
bribe to cover up the crime of a colleague; the affair came
to light, and the ruler had the offender beaten severely,
after which the official supervising the punishment cut
out the culprit's heart and ate a piece of his flesh.[39]

Later, Goody adds: "In the Guan and Ming periods human flesh
again appeared as an item of diet and we hear of steamed
dumplings filled with minced humans."[40]

   The connection between estrangement of husband and wife
and the experience of metaphoric cannibalism in male/female
confrontation is evident in Marge Piercy's *Small Changes*. "The
Book of Beth" describes the marriage, its disintegration and the
new life Beth forges for herself. In her wedding dress, Beth felt
like a wedding cake: they would come and slice her and take her
home ... Jim's love-making after their marriage was unfulfilling
for Beth:

> She felt much less satisfied than she had after one of
> those fumbling long-drawn-out sessions on the couch or
> the back seat of his Chevy. It was accomplished. That
> was it, the whole thing. They had made love finally, but
> where was the love they had made?.[41]

The relationship deteriorated further. She felt as if Jim had
developed jagged spikes that stuck out into her, so that she must
retract not to encounter them. He became "spinier and more
angular"; she became "smaller and denser".[42] "He was
expanding and she was contracting."[43] To domesticate her into
motherhood, Jim flushed her birth-control pills down the toilet.
Afraid of fighting him and fearful of conceiving his child, which
she perceived as a trap, Beth experienced the emotions of an
animal that is first trapped then devoured:

> ... after a while she began to eat, chewing the meat loaf a
> bite at a time. A trapped animal eating a dead animal.
> She chewed and swallowed. He was willing to trap her.
> That made him the enemy.[44]

Jim made some half-hearted efforts to console Beth, but the taint of
cannibalism remained:

> He had meant well, he said he loved her, though she had
> grown so mistrustful of that word she did not think she
> would ever again be able to use it except as she might
> say, I love to swim, or I love strawberries. *I love to eat up
> Bethie. Bethie is mine.* No, she would steal his property
> from him and belong to no one but herself.[45]

The revulsion toward eating flesh, from the night of the meat loaf,
endured:

> It was part superstition and part morality: she had
> escaped to her freedom and did not want to steal the life
> of other warm-blooded creatures. She ate brown rice and
> whole-grain breads and granola and muesli and

cracked wheat and lentils and navy, lima, mung,
marrow, kidney, and turtle beans.[46]

An awareness of Jim's predatory appetite and her own
vulnerability to his advances grew on her slowly. As she felt a
slow erosion of her personhood, she perceived the steadily opposite
effect in Jim. He dilated in size as he aggrandized her rights and
assimilated her identity to serve his needs. The devouring by her
of animal flesh was equivalent in her mind to the same violent act
inflicted on her by Jim. She "cannibalized" animals, while he
cannibalized her.

Where do we go from here? How do we cease to perceive one
gender as food and the other as consuming it? How do we raise the
consciousness of males from woman-as-cookie-jar to woman as
human? How do we raise the consciousness of females above a
masochistic pleasure in participating in their own edibility?

Judy Chicago's "The Dinner Party", 1973, is one monumental
effort in this direction. Using the metaphor of women as food and
more specifically the vagina as feast, "The Dinner Party" proposes
a triangular dining table, ancient symbol of the vagina, each wing
forty and a half feet long, laid out with thirty-nine sculptured
vagina-like dishes, to celebrate the achievements of thirty-nine
women from prehistoric times to the present. The first wing of the
table goes from prehistory (goddess myths) to the decline of Greco-
Roman culture (Hypatia); the second goes from Christianity
(Marcella) to the Reformation (Anna van Schurman); the last goes
from the 17th to the 20th centuries (Anne Hutchinson to Georgia
O'Keeffe). It is a tour of Western Civilization that treads a road
little traveled, the road of female achievements. It is a feast unique
in its diners, in that it is women celebrating their own gender.

Curiously, Chicago's original idea for "The Dinner Party" was
to commemorate twenty-five women who were eaten alive.
Changing the thrust of her art-work from negative to affirmative
symbols, Chicago altered the original idea. In its place she
celebrates the first supper for women, in contrast with the biblical
last supper, which commemorates, according to Chicago, a
patriarchal Christianity. The vaginal dishes are not intended to
reduce women to cunts, as some thought, but to make her
femininity holy. The swelling pods straining out of dishes are
reminiscent of the fertility powers of early goddesses. The
chalices, again symbolic of the vagina, are a sacrament to her
femininity. Woman is on her own turn hallowed in her femininity
and celebrant of her own movable feast. Thus, in a very real sense

"The Dinner Party" is goddess-food, not the flesh and blood of thirst in holy communion, but the flesh and blood of woman with a capital "W".

Woman has made a start in returning herself to her own self. She will, as Andrea Dworkin puts it, "serve *herself*, instead of serving herself up like turkey or duck, garnished, stuffed, sharpened knife ready for ritual carving".[47] Let us hold hands and break bread in thanks - the banquet usurped from us is now our own. Ceres lives!

Eira Patnaik

NOTES

[1] Ed. Cray, *The Anthology of Restoration Erotic Poetry*, North Hollywood: Brandon House, 1965, p. 88.

[2] Ibid., p. 65.

[3] Ibid., p. 63.

[4] Ibid., p. 41.

[5] Una Stannard, "The Mask of Beauty", *Woman in Sexist Society*, ed. Vivian Gormick and Barbara K. Moran, New York: Basic Books, 1971, p. 124.

[6] See, for example, John Ruskin, *Sesame and Lilies*, New York: John Wiley & Sons, 1872, p. 145.

[7] *Woman in Sexist Society*, p. 124.

[8] Jane Thornypine, "A Dangerous Woman", *Harper's Magazine*, April 1866, p. 620.

[9] Elinor Wylie, *Collected Prose of Elinor Wylie*, New York: Alfred Knopf, 1934, p. 87.

[10] Ibid., p. 50.

[11] Ibid., p. 199.

[12] Ibid., p. 203.

[13] M.E. Sherwood, "New England Woman", *Atlantic Monthly*, August 1878, p. 230.

[14] Harold Wentworth and Stuart Berg Flexner, *Dictionary of American Slang*, New York: Thomas B. Crowell, 1975, p. xiii.

[15] Benjamin Walker, *Man and Beasts Within*, New York: Stein & Day, 1977, p. 143.

[16] Ibid., p. 72.

[17] Conroy Maddox, *Dali*, New York: Crown Publishers, 1978, p. 29.
[18] Jean Brillat-Savarin, *The Physiology of Taste or Meditations on Transcendental Gastronomy*, New York: Alfred Knopf, 1971, p. 4.
[19] Jack Goody, *Cooking, Cuisine and Class*, London: Cambridge University Press, 1982, p. 114.
[20] Tennessee Williams, *Collected Stories*, New York: New Directions Books, 1985, pp. 65-66.
[21] Ibid., p. 69.
[22] Marge Piercy, *Small Changes*, New York: Fawcett Crest, 1972, p. 80.
[23] Otto Weininger, *Sex and Character*, New York: Putnam & Sons, 1975, p. 286.
[24] Fay Weldon, *The Fat Woman's Joke*, London: Macgibbon & Kee, 1967, p. 49.
[25] Ibid.
[26] Milton Rugoff, *The Travels of Marco Polo*, New York: New American Library, 1961, pp. 183-4.
[27] Ibid., p. 184.
[28] Magnus Pyke, *Food and Society*, London: Cox & Wyman, 1968, p. 11.
[29] Ibid., p. 10.
[30] Margaret Atwood, *The Edible Woman*, New York: Warner Books, 1983, p. 250.
[31] Ibid.
[32] Ibid., p. 251.
[33] Ibid., p. 235.
[34] Ibid., p. 275.
[35] Ibid., p. 276.
[36] Ibid., pp. 277-8.
[37] Ibid., p. 279.
[38] *Cooking, Cuisine and Class*, p. 107.
[39] Ibid.
[40] Ibid.
[41] *Small Changes*, p. 12.
[42] Ibid., p. 33.
[43] Ibid.
[44] Ibid., p. 41.
[45] Ibid., p. 45 (my emphasis).
[46] Ibid., p. 48.
[47] Andrea Dworkin, *Woman Hating*, New York: E.P. Dutton, 1974, p. 70.

7.

FREUDIAN GASTRONOMY IN MARIO VARGAS LLOSA'S *LA CIUDAD Y LOS PERROS*

On numerous occasions Mario Vargas Llosa has emphasized the seminal role that "demons" play in shaping a novelist's works, most notably in the second chapter of *Gabriel García Márquez: historia de un deicidio*.[1] Vargas Llosa's own "demons" - personal, historical and cultural - are by now legendary: his father, Odría, Flaubert, *Tirant lo Blanc*, Western democracy, hippopotamuses and jogging to name but a few. But Vargas Llosa's *paparazzi* know of another one: a passion for gastronomy which he indulges publicly during his regular visits to Madrid, Paris, New York and other cities renowned for their cuisine.

Ever mindful of his waistline, however, Vargas Llosa nowadays is more likely to be seen savouring a grilled *rape* on the Costa del Sol than wolfing down a *fabada* in Oviedo. On the other hand, he imposes no such culinary restraint upon his novelistic characters. In *Pantaleón y las visitadoras* Tigre Collazos, Coronel López López and General Victoria gorge themselves on a stupendous banquet of Peruvian delights that defy translation: *anticuchos, choclos sancochados, escabeche de pato con ají, cebiche de corvina, riñoncitos a la criolla con arroz blanco, alfajores de miel* and *maní*.[2] Throughout *Conversación en La Catedral* Zavalita is only ever stirred out of his existential aboulia by the flavour and aroma of a *chupe de camarones* (prawn stew).[3] In *El hablador* the fictional Vargas Llosa farewells his friend Mascarita over a mountain of *sandwichs de chicharrón* (crackling sandwiches) and *mazamorra morada* (a typical Peruvian dish of boiled maize).[4] The reader's mouth waters even as he winces at the harrowing reality of Peru, *jodido* and *malhadado*,[5] depicted in Vargas Llosa's fiction.

Overall, the gastronomic episodes in Vargas Llosa's fictional representation of his sad country serve two principal functions: first, they heighten an unmistakeably Peruvian setting and atmosphere and, second, they demonstrate that, irrespective of the depths of degradation to which their personal or national fortunes may sink, Peruvians will always manage to find solace in the delights of their national cuisine: *la comida criolla*. Vargas Llosa's novels and plays demonstrate that whatever their foibles, failings and infelicities, Peruvians can at least impress the rest of the world with their inventive gastronomy and their unflinching enjoyment of it.

However, there is one notorious and still more significant episode in Vargas Llosa's very first novel, *La ciudad y los perros*, which does not fit into the general gastronomic scheme outlined above - I refer to the raping, slaughtering, cooking and eating of a hen by four cadets - Cavas, Boa, Jaguar and Rulos.[6] Critics are correct in interpreting the episode - as well as the other grotesque sexual episodes in the novel - as a violent, primitive response by the repressed, frustrated cadets to the tactics of physical, moral and spiritual "bastardization" employed against them by the military system embodied in Leoncio Prado.[7] But a further question facing the reader is whether there is any particular significance attached to the fact that in this instance the target of the boys' sexual violence should be a hen ...

It is now well established that Freud constitutes one of Vargas Llosa's most potent "cultural" demons.[8] Accordingly, the significance of the hen is clarified if the grotesque episode is read in the light of a case cited in *Totem and Taboo*, a celebrated book in which Freud draws suggestive analogies between the attitude of children to animals and of primitive men to their totem animals. Freud discusses the case of a two-and-a-half-year-old boy, little Arpad, who has had his penis bitten by a fowl; the consequence of this mishap is that he becomes obsessed with poultry, his favourite pastime being their slaughter. To quote from *Totem and Taboo*:

> The slaughtering of poultry was a regular festival for him. He would dance round the animals' bodies for hours at a time in a state of intense excitement. But afterwards he would kiss and stroke the slaughtered animal or would clean and caress the toy fowls that he had himself ill-treated.[9]

In this particular instance, little Arpad gave the vital clues to the Oedipal significance of his phobia: on one occasion he declared "My father's the cock"; on another, "Now I'm small, now I'm a chicken. When I get bigger I'll be a fowl. When I'm bigger still I'll be a cock"; subsequently he confided he would like to eat "fricassée of mother" and, finally, one day he came out with the declaration: "I'll marry my mother".[10] From the analysis of this case, Freud came to the conclusion that the totem animal is identified as the father by the boy and that in slaughtering the fowls he was symbolically killing the father so that he could possess the mother. Freud goes on to argue:

> If the totem animal is the father, then the two principal ordinances of totemism, the two taboo prohibitions which constitute its core - not to kill the totem and not to have sexual relations with a woman of the same totem - coincide in their content with the two crimes of Oedipus, who killed his father and married his mother, as well as with the two primal wishes of children, the insufficient repression or the re-awakening of which forms the nucleus of perhaps every psychoneurosis.[11]

In view of Freud's conclusions arising from the analysis of the case involving little Arpad and other similar cases, and given the Oedipal basis of the psychological problems disturbing the principal adolescent characters in the novel, it is feasible to argue that in their ceremonial raping, slaughtering and eating of the hen, Cavas, Boa, Jaguar and Rulos are symbolically abusing and killing their fathers; in other words, they are symbolically re-enacting their own individual parricidal battles - and by extension, the parricidal battles of other cadets in Leoncio Prado.

The parricidal connotations of the rape and slaughter of the hen are further illuminated by the suggestive parallels that the episode bears with Freud's description in *Totem and Taboo* of totemic festivals, in which primitive societies commemorate the "memorable and criminal deed" which comprises the historical, collective origin of the Oedipus complex: the first parricide or slaughter of the primal father by the jealous, rebellious sons of the primal horde.[12] Imaginatively (and controversially) linking individual and social psychology by drawing an analogy between boys like little Arpad regarding an animal as their father and primitive men identifying their totem animals with the primal father, Freud goes on to observe: "the clan is celebrating the ceremonial occasion by the cruel slaughter of its totem animal and is devouring it raw - blood, flesh and bones".[13] The "cruel slaughter" in the totemic ritual corresponds with the dismemberment of the hen while it is still alive by the four cadets in the novel: "... Yo ni sé como se mata ... La agarras del pescuezo y la tuerces en el aire ... Sí señor, la elevaste, bien puesta esa pata. Ahora si se ha muerto, está toda deshecha, caramba".[14] The clan devours the totem animal raw, the cadets suck its bones and eat its flesh: "Puaf, decía el Rulos, chupando un hueso, la carne ha quedado toda chamuscada y con pelos".[15]

Freud explains that during the totemic slaughter and meal:
"each man is conscious that he is performing an act forbidden to
the individual and justifiable only through the participation of the
whole clan; nor may anyone absent himself from the killing and
the meal".[16] In the novel, each of the boys knows that he is
engaging in a forbidden activity and for that reason they seek the
cover of darkness, try to silence the hen and are on the lookout for
any officers or guards:

> ¡Tápale el pico, jijunagrandísima! Teniente Gamboa,
> aquí hay alguien que se está comiendo una gallina.
> Son las diez o casi, dijo el Rulos, más de las diez y
> cuarto. ¿Han visto si hay imaginarias?.[17]

The clan consciousness described by Freud in the totemic ritual is
paralleled by the solidarity of the four boys involved, all of whom
are members of their own clan, "el Círculo" (the Circle), which
was formed to protect themselves against rival groups of cadets.
In the totemic ritual, according to Freud, the "slaughtered animal
is lamented and bewailed. The mourning is obligatory, imposed by
dread of a threatened retribution".[18] Similarly, in the episode of
the hen, a ritualistic lamentation is suggested by the cadets'
rhythmic repetition: "está toda deshecha, caramba. Caramba,
está toda deshecha"; their fear of retribution is conveyed by the
furtiveness with which they participate in the prank. Indeed, like
the members of the primitive clan described in *Totem and Taboo*,
the four cadets appear to be taking part in a grotesque festival in
which every instinct is unfettered and there is licence for every
kind of gratification.

The primitive savagery of the clan in *Totem and Taboo* is
conveyed in the novel not only by the barbarity of the episode, but
also by such totemic-sounding names as Jaguar (in honour of the
feline whose ferocity he shares) and Boa (in honour of the snake
which he resembles in the uncommon length of his penis). Cavas
is a highland Indian with typically short, stubby hair, who is
taunted for looking like the "last of the Mohicans"; in view of the
analogies already drawn with the cannibal savages of *Totem and
Taboo*, it could well be that Vargas Llosa gave him the name Cavas
because of its phonetic echoes of "cuevas" (caves), which in turn
evokes images of "hombre de las cuevas" (caveman), whose
behaviour is aped by the cadets. Moreover, the primitive-sounding
gibberish of the cadets in the section dealing simultaneously with
the rape of the hen and the would-be rape of "el gordito" (a chubby

cadet), dramatizes their apparent reversion to barbarism: "Uf ... Uf ... jijunagrandísima ... Puaf".[19]

In *Totem and Taboo* Freud links individual and social psychology. Similarly, in *La ciudad y los perros* a double psychological layer may be discerned in the episode of the hen. Just as the cadets are reenacting their own individual parricidal battles, the episode symbolizes the collective struggle of the cadets against the military officers of Leoncio Prado. Its wider social significance is suggested by the fact that a gang is involved in the rape and slaughter of the hen; and if it is accepted that the hen is a father symbol at an individual level, it then follows that it also stands as a symbol of the authoritarian, paternalistic, military system personified by the Colonel. Indeed, the hen is an apt symbol for the short, fat Colonel with a high-pitched voice; and his hysterical behaviour during the madcap episode of "la prueba de la soga" (the tug of war) is reminiscent of the terrified flapping of the hen. Moreover, the parallel between the hen and the Colonel extends to the grotesquely comic analogy that just as the hen's sexual "honour" is violated, so the Colonel's military "honour" is defiled during the episode of the "prueba de la soga", as suggested by Boa's derisory comment: "lo fundimos delante del ministro, delante de los embajadores, dicen que (el coronel) casi lloraba".[20] For the Colonel, Leoncio Prado represents his "family", and the cadets are his surrogate "sons". Thus, in the military school the adolescent cadets are pitted against a brutally repressive father figure who tries to turn them into monkeys: in Boa's indignant words, "qué es eso de exhibirnos como monos".[21] The cadets in their turn transform the Colonel into a hen, and its rape, slaughter and devouring may be interpreted as a collective, symbolical rebellion against the tyrannical "father". In Freudian terms, the four cadets, in the name of the "clan" of which they are leading members, are displacing onto the hen the pent-up resentment and hostility against the military system. Individual parricidal struggles are thus reenacted on a collective level. The cadets as a group, figuratively at least, triumph in their own battle against paternalistic authority: the grotesque prank played upon the hapless hen symbolizes what the cadets would like to do to the Colonel!

Roy Boland

NOTES

[1] Mario Vargas Llosa, *Gabriel García Márquez: historia de un deicidio*, Barcelona: Barral Editores, 1971. In the controversial second chapter of this book, Vargas Llosa describes his theory of the "demons" and applies it to García Márquez's fiction.

[2] Mario Vargas Llosa, *Pantaleón y las visitadoras*, Barcelona: Seix Barral, 1973, p. 242.

[3] Mario Vargas Llosa, *Conversación en La Catedral*, Barcelona: Seix Barral, 1969. See, for example, pp. 15, 295 and 656.

[4] Mario Vargas Llosa, *El hablador*, Barcelona: Seix Barral, 1987. See p. 100.

[5] *Jodido* (fucked) is the epithet describing Peru that runs through *Conversación en La Catedral*; *malhadado* (star-crossed) is the adjective employed to describe Peru in the opening sentence of *El hablador*.

[6] Mario Vargas Llosa, *La ciudad y los perros*, Barcelona: Seix Barral, 1963, pp. 34-38.

[7] See, for example, José Miguel Oviedo, *Mario Vargas Llosa: La invención de una realidad*, Barcelona: Seix Barral, 1982, pp. 100-2.

[8] For Vargas Llosa's indebtedness to Freud, see "Entrevista a Mario Vargas Llosa por Roland Forgues", in Michel Moner, *Les avatars de la première personne et le moi balbutiant de "La tía Julia y el escribidor"*, Toulouse: France-Ibérie Recherche, 1983, pp. 73-74. The Freudian layer of Vargas Llosa's novels is also the subject of my own *Oedipus and the "Papa State". A Study of Individual and Social Psychology in Mario Vargas Llosa's Novels of Peruvian Reality from "La ciudad y los perros" to "Historia de Mayta"*, Madrid: Editorial Voz, 1988.

[9] Sigmund Freud, *Totem and Taboo*, London: Ark Paperbacks, 1983, p. 130.

[10] Ibid., pp. 130-1.

[11] Ibid., p. 132.

[12] Ibid., pp. 140-2.

[13] Ibid., p. 140.

[14] *La ciudad y los perros*, p. 37. "I don't even know how to kill her ... You grab her, wring her neck and swing her around ... That's it, you've done it, what good footwork you've got. It's really dead now, bloody hell, what a revolting mess."

[15] Ibid., p. 38. "Ugh", said Rulos, chewing at a bone, "the flesh is all burnt and it's full of feathers."

[16] *Totem and Taboo*, p. 140.

[17] *La ciudad y los perros*, p. 36. "Shut its beak, fucking bitch! Lieutenant Gamboa, here's somebody screwing a hen. It's almost ten, no, it's after a quarter past. Have you checked if there's any guards around the place?"

[18] *Totem and Taboo*, p. 140.

[19] *La ciudad y los perros*, pp. 35-38.

[20] Ibid., p. 73. "We stuffed him up in front of the Minister, in front of the

Ambassadors, they say that (the Colonel) almost burst into tears."
[21] Ibid., p. 73. "How dare he? showing us off as if we were monkeys!"

8.

CULINARY REVELATIONS: SELF-EXPLORATION AND FOOD
IN MARGARET LAURENCE'S *THE STONE ANGEL*

Old Meg she was a gypsy,
And lived upon the moors;
Her bed it was the brown heath-turf,
And her house was out of doors.

Her apples were swart blackberries,
Her currants, pods o' broom;
Her wine was dew of the wild white rose,
Her book a churchyard tomb. ...

No breakfast had she many a morn,
No dinner many a noon,
And 'stead of supper, she would stare
Full hard against the moon!

So does Keats write of Meg Merrilies in his lyric of the same name, yet the description is perhaps as fittingly applied to Hagar Shipley, the protagonist of Margaret Laurence's *The Stone Angel*. In fact, midway through the novel, Hagar remarks: "I'm like Meg Merrilies"[1] and goes on to catalogue the similarity in their diets. In a short, well-argued essay, Joan Coldwell[2] has already explored the resemblance between Laurence's protagonist and the madwoman of ballad and folklore fame. Flowers and berries ultimately become the regenerative staples of both women's diets as they try to find a healthy, female existence in the world defined and controlled by men. Both are wanderers in search of their respective "homes". Indeed, it should be recalled that at the heart of all five of Laurence's Manawaka novels is this search for a home, for a sense of community, a sense of belonging, a sense of identity.[3] Unwilling to become a "mad Madge" figure, Hagar Shipley reconstructs her story and her self in her tale of "the stone angel". Consciously, she tells her story of isolation and recounts how she became the "stone angel" of the title choosing art rather than life, civilization over the wilderness, the artificial rather than the real. Unconsciously, however, she is transformed from the stone angel into a true, nourishing, female. Although Hagar

herself is unaware of this change, through an examination of the
food patterns, the reader can see and understand the
metamorphosis. Thus, by the conclusion of her tale, Hagar has
become the nurturing angel; she is able to define herself as female
and assume the mothering role, if only briefly, before her death.

Afraid of her "disorderly", wild emotions, Hagar, throughout
her ninety years, has restrained herself within a code of
respectability and repression. She has come to share in her
father's Victorian beliefs and thus despises her very femininity.
Considering it a weakness, she has refused to acquiesce to her
womanliness and never becomes, therefore, the angel in the
house,[4] offering succour and food to others; instead she remains
the fossilized figure found in the cemetery. In fact, as she begins
her narrative, Hagar reflects that, internally, she has become
noticeably stone-like: constipation is her primary affliction. She is
burdened with food and with life: "my belly growls and snarls like
a separate beast. My bowels are locked today. I am Job in
reverse," she tells us. "I sit uncomfortably, I am bloated, full,
weighted down, and I fear I may pass wind".[5] In an effort to
diagnose her interior disorder, Hagar undergoes a series of X-
rays. Tricked into drinking the barium, she realizes that "It goes
through my head now that the pit of hell might be similar to this.
... I only wish my stomach or whatever it is could be left alone".[6]
But it cannot be; her interior self is scrutinized like her stomach in
order to determine what her affliction truly is.

The affliction is, it may be argued, lack of self-giving, lack of
self-definition; it is an acceptance of a "self" given to her by the
patriarchal community. Because of her affiliation with her father
at varying times during the course of her life, Hagar denies her
role as woman, wife, and mother. Laurence explores this
conscious denial in the rhetorical language of food. On one level,
the novel is laced with food epithets and comparisons: for
example, in the first pages, we learn that the cemetery is "thick
and rich as syrup",[7] that Regina Weese, a totally self-sacrificing
woman with an angel monument, was "bland as egg custard".[8]
As Hagar continues her journey, most especially in the second
half of the novel, she is described more and more like a threatened,
even edible, animal: from the fattened calf to the seagulls, to an
old hawk that is caught, to being ignominiously hauled up like a
fish in a net, to the final state of being tied in bed like a trussed
fowl. Such metaphoric comparisons are apt in the disjunction
they contain, for Hagar wants to view herself less and less like a
woman and become more and more the stone angel her father
adores.

On a second, more significant level, Laurence consciously and meticulously casts Hagar's unconscious search for a true feminine self in terms of an extended food odyssey. Like the Victorians themselves, and it should be recalled that Hagar is herself a late Victorian child,[9] Hagar's life is circumscribed between two contradictory poles; it is to rid herself of this tension between the artificial and the real, between male definitions of the female and those decided upon by the woman herself, that Hagar escapes. Each flight involves movement away from one male and towards another, together with an attempt at traditional, female succouring - a catering to the male definition of the angel in the house. In each case, Hagar's attempt to move from the paralysed image of the stone angel to the nourishing angel of the house is met with frustration and with denial. Because she is following male-imposed, not self-generated definitions, she is untrue to herself. Her freedom comes only at the end, after her cathartic meal at Shadow Point, when she is in the hospital. For she turns from male-produced selfishness to feminine selflesssness as she comes to the aid of Sandra Wong.

Each attempt to define herself involves Hagar in a movement from civilization to wilderness, to what is unknown outside the male-defined world. In her presentation of this Laurence constantly pits what is artificial against what is natural; it is only in the uncultivated meal that Hagar will begin to find herself. Borrowing Lévi-Strauss's terminology, Hagar must move away from cooked, meat-meals (men's food) toward a lighter, raw diet (woman's fare), if she is to complete successfully her search for self. She must force from herself all male definitions of (her)self that are encumbered with the male ideology of food and its role.

Farb and Armelagos have succinctly noted the importance of food and gender when they observe: "In all societies, both simple and complex, eating is the primary way of initiating and maintaining human relationships".[10] Nowhere, surely, is this more apparent than in the relationship of mothering. Food ultimately comes to mean mother, Harriet Moore tells us in an interesting essay in the *American Journal of Clinical Nutrition*: "Feeding is not only kindly and warm in its emotional meaning to the one who accepts, but he is most likely to see the giver as somehow glossed over with the meaning of 'mother'".[11] The gender roles hold true: the provider is considered masculine, while the cook/nourisher is feminine. Indeed the entire process of civilisation, then, can be viewed as a gender issue, for it is the female who transforms the raw, natural food into a civilized, cooked meal.[12] It is thus that Hagar approaches her initial association with, and later marriage to, Bram Shipley: "I - thought he looked a bearded Indian so brown and beaked a face. ... The next instant, though, I imagined him rigged out in a suit of gray soft as a dove's breast feathers".[13] But she is unsuccessful - both because Bram won't allow himself to be "civilized", but more importantly because Hagar is trying to cook-seduce him to a position that is antithetical to her own nature. Hagar runs away from her father, from Bram, from Mr Oatley, and finally from Marvin because she cannot mother/feed them; she cannot do so because Hagar, until her ninetieth year, cannot truly feed/mother herself. She does not yet know herself ...

Hagar's first step toward self-knowledge comes when she runs away from the highly civilized and rigid patriarchal life which her father offers. She rebels and "marries below" her, accepting the disreputable yet sexually vital Bram Shipley. Hagar incorrectly thought that she could "tame" and transform him ... Little girls, Hagar remembers, were taught the art of civilizing the beast that is man through their culinary magic. Sent to a young ladies' academy in Toronto, Hagar learned "embroidery, and French, and menu-planning for a five-course meal, and poetry, and how to take a firm hand with servants".[14] Using that ideology articulated by Lévi-Strauss in his *The Raw and the Cooked*, Laurence has Hagar attempt to become the nourisher of her husband and her two sons. She cooks meat and tries to civilize them, but, as this passage makes clear, she can do so only by being untrue to herself:

> I'd pass the plates to them, serve them all before I ate
> myself, watch them wolf down fried potatoes and apple
> pie for breakfast, never letting on how I felt about it,
> Hagar Currie serving a bunch of breeds and ne'er-do-
> wells and Galicians.[15]

She cannot find the balance between the male-articulated civilization and the feminine wilderness, appropriately symbolized by the "honeyed butcher knife"[16] Bram offers to his son John. During her marriage, Hagar is transformed - not into the succouring, nourishing angel, but instead into a denial of the female self, into the Stone Angel. Unable to feed herself raw, female food, she eats civilized food and becomes increasingly one of them:

> I stood for a long time, looking, wondering how a person
> could change so much and never see it. ... I was
> wearing a man's black overcoat that ... bunched and

> pulled up on front, for I'd put on weight on my hips, and
> my stomach had never gone flat again after John was
> born. ... My hair was gray and straight. I always cut it
> myself. The face - a brown and leathery face that
> wasn't mine. Only the eyes were mine, staring as
> though to pierce the lying glass and get beneath to some
> truer image, infinitely distant.[17]

Hagar's male-like appearance is contrasted with the saccharine, feminine Lottie when they have tea together. However, Laurence also underscores the discrepancies between the falsely civilized female and the true female (though, in Hagar's case, still in an unformed state). Lottie has accepted the male definitions of the female; Hagar has not.

It is not surprising, therefore, that she soon runs away to become the housekeeper/cook for Mr Oatley. However, such "succouring", for a wage this time, is not of long duration. Hagar cannot continue to feed a male who:

> ... used to bring Oriental wives here ... and charge huge
> sums for passage, and pack the females like tinned
> shrimp in the lower hold, and if the Immigration men
> scented the hoax, the false bottom was levered open, and
> the women plummeted.[18]

Oatley, like Jason Currie and Bram Shipley, does not value the female. Hagar cannot feed this man, and she flees once again, this time returning to Bram's deathbed. When Hagar returns to the Shipley place, the house, the kitchen especially, is less than welcoming. Laurence's symbolism is pointed here: the kitchen is a metaphor of Hagar's failed culinary, mothering role:

> ... the house had that rancid smell that comes from
> unwashed dishes and sour floors and food left sitting on
> the table. The kitchen was a shambles. You could have
> scratched your initials in the dark grease that coated the
> oilcloth on the table. A loaf of bread sat there with the
> butcher knife stuck into it like a spear. A dish of stewed
> saskatoons, the berries hard and small, was being
> attended by a court of flies. On a larded piece of salt
> pork a mammoth Matriarchal fly was labouring
> obscenely to squeeze out of herself her white clustered
> eggs.[19]

Unlike the "Matriarchal fly", Hagar has no eggs at all, no mothering, civilizing urges to leave or to return to. And it is John who presides over Bram's deathbed, a substitute for Hagar.

The third escape, and the one that occupies the greatest part of the novel, is her running away from her son, Marvin, and his wife, Doris, and from their efforts to place her in the Silverthreads Nursing Home. It is this escape which finally proves liberating and self-freeing for Hagar; she runs away from the false mothering that the nursing home provides and also escapes from the "maternal" care that Doris gives her.

Even at this point, Hagar is still the stone angel - she tells us that she sat on the bus "Rigid as marble ... solid and stolid to outward view".[20] But as she approaches Shadow Point, and her rendezvous with herself, she sheds these layers of the civilized Hagar. Indeed, she has even changed clothes and does not wear her usual style of dress. Even more importantly, she feeds herself, only herself, during this escape. She buys special food for Shadow Point:

> A box of soda biscuits, the salted kind - Doris always
> buys those bland, unsalted ones that I don't like. A little
> tin of jam, greengage, my favorite. Some large bars of
> plain milk chocolate, very nourishing ... a packet of
> those small cheeses.[21]

And she likens herself, significantly, to the famous, bewitched, Meg Merrilies.[22] She makes herself into just such a character, complete with a June bug crown: "They liven my gray, transform me. I sit quite still and straight, my hands spread languidly on my knees, queen of moth-millers, express of earwigs".[23] In her royal state, Hagar begins the final, cathartic, but necessary journey with all its Christian overtones that will lead her to herself. Naturally enough, this last journey also involves a meal with a man, Murray Ferney Lees, the Dependable Life Assurance man. But it is a meal unlike any other in which Hagar has participated. It involves no cooked, civilizing meat; she does not prepare it, but they just sort of spontaneously share their odd communion of cheap wine and salted crackers. Slightly drunk, Hagar, for the first and last time, tells the story of her son John, his death and her subsequent turning to stone. She finally sees herself as both the ministering and the stone angel. The story is cleansing and concludes with Hagar's vomiting the non-nutritious contents of her al fresco picnic. With the expulsion, comes peace.

The remainder of the story - her placement in the nursing home, the soothing pills and increasing "hazy lethargy"[24] together with the bland, soft diet which she is fed in the hospital - adds little to the self-revelation that has taken place. However, because Hagar is fed such a woman's diet and because she eats it, Laurence is able to point out that by the end, Hagar has found her feminine self. Her act of kindness to Sandra and her telling Marvin that he was a "better son than John",[25] together with her final murmuring of the mother-words - "There, There"[26] - complete Hagar's journey, and she is allowed to slip quietly into the medicinal cocoon prepared for her. No longer needing food for her journey, she is left only with a glass of water which she holds for herself. Like Meg Merrilies, she no longer needs breakfast, dinner, or supper. Unwilling to engage in the centuries' old male notion of woman as cook, Hagar refuses to domesticate the wilderness for man, and instead turns to her own inner wilderness in an effort to tame herself, to stare at her own moon.

Mary Anne Schofield

NOTES

[1] Margaret Laurence, *The Stone Angel*, New York: Bantam Books, 1981, p. 134.

[2] Joan Coldwell, "Hagar as Meg Merrilies, the Homeless Gipsy", *Journal of Canadian Fiction*, no. 27 (1979), pp. 92-100.

[3] See Theo Q. Dombrowski, "Who is this You? Margaret Laurence and Identity", *University of Windsor Review*, no. 13, pp. 21-38.

[4] The phrase, "the angel in the house", was first used by Coventry Patmore (1823-1896) in his long poem of the same name, designed to be the apotheosis of married love. In today's critical rhetoric, it has come to symbolize all the characteristics associated with Victorian feminism: mothering, frailty, softness, caring. In her article, "A Feminist Reading of *The Stone Angel*", *Canadian Literature*, no. 93, pp. 26-41, Constance Rooke argues that Hagar's progress can be charted in terms of her movement towards and away from the image of the sepulchral stone angel. She notes on page 27: "Hagar has supplanted her mother, rejected her image, and chosen instead to mirror her father's pride. But in the shadow of that stone angel which she becomes is another angel, ministering and mild - the kind of woman we take her mother to have been."

[5] *The Stone Angel*, p. 34.

[6] Ibid., pp. 97-98.

[7] Ibid., p. 2.

[8] Ibid.

[9] See Harriet Blodgett, "The Real Lives of Margaret Laurence's Women", *Critique. Studies in Modern Fiction*, no. 23, pp. 5-17.

[10] Peter Farb and George Armelagos, *Consuming Passions. The Anthropology of Eating*, Boston: Houghton Mifflin Co., 1980, p. 3.

[11] Harriet Moore, "The Meaning of Food", *American Journal of Clinical Nutrition*, no. 5, p. 79.

[12] See Claude Lévi-Strauss, *The Raw and the Cooked*, Chicago: University Press, 1969, passim.

[13] *The Stone Angel*, p. 39.

[14] Ibid., p. 36.

[15] Ibid., pp. 100-1.

[16] Ibid., p. 110.

[17] Ibid., p. 111.

[18] Ibid., p. 138.

[19] Ibid., p. 151.

[20] Ibid., p. 129.

[21] Ibid., p. 131.

[22] Ibid., p. 134.

[23] Ibid., p. 193.

[24] Ibid., p. 233.

[25] Ibid., p. 272.

[26] Ibid., p. 275.

9.

J.M. COETZEE'S *MICHAEL K*: STARVING IN A LAND OF PLENTY

The fragrance of the burning flesh rose into the sky. Speaking the words he had been taught, directing them no longer upward but to the earth on which he knelt, he prayed: "For what we are about to receive make us truly thankful". With two wire skewers he turned the strips, and in mid-act felt his heart suddenly flow over with thankfulness. It was exactly as they had described it, like a gush of warm water. Now it is completed, he said to himself. All that remains is to live here quietly for the rest of my life, eating the food that my own labour has made the earth to yield. All that remains is to be a tender of the soil. He lifted the first strip to his mouth. Beneath the crisply charred skin the flesh was soft and juicy. He chewed with tears of joy in his eyes. The best, he thought, the very best pumpkin I have tasted.[1]

It is quite obvious from this fragment that eating the food he has grown himself is to Michael K, the central character in J.M. Coetzee's *Life and Times of Michael K*, the Booker-prize winner of 1983, the realization of his ultimate goal. Indeed, this meal provides the only joy Michael ever experiences in the novel. Although it is had in the most appalling of circumstances, it is nonetheless of crucial significance to Michael and constitutes the climax of his life. Michael's enjoyment of it provides a basic clue to his personality and to the interpretation of the novel.

The story is set in an imaginary future; the place is a recognizable South Africa where a civil war is raging. The situation in Cape Town, where Michael works as a gardener, has become desperate. In a city swamped with war refugees chaos reigns. Michael's mother, who is ill, longs to go back to the farm near Prince Albert in the Karoo, a barren desert-like region in the South African interior where she spent a happy youth. In her fantasy Prince Albert is transformed into a garden of Eden, "a time of warmth and plenty".[2] Out of fear of starvation they finally decide to leave for Prince Albert without waiting any longer for the necessary official documents. Michael transports his mother and their belongings on a makeshift wheelbarrow. On the way, in Stellenbosch, his mother dies and is cremated. Michael, however, is undeterred and carries on, without knowing why, but with the intuitive conviction that he has a mission to complete.

Indeed, after arriving at the farm which has been abandoned by its owner and while burying his mother's ashes in the soil, he discovers his calling: to make the earth fruitful by planting and tending seeds. Michael starts a garden and from then onwards his whole life revolves around it. When a deserter arrives at the farm, Michael is forced to leave. He hides out in the mountains, but has to return to Prince Albert, sick with starvation. He is interned in a labour camp but after a while escapes and returns to the farm. Once more he starts growing pumpkins and melons and this time is fortunate enough to savour the fruits he has cultivated. Not long afterwards he is discovered by an army patrol, taken for a suspected guerilla contact, and sent to a rehabilitation camp in Kenilworth, Cape Town. His stay in the camp, the second part of the book, is related by the medical officer who is very much intrigued and puzzled by Michael K.

The short, final part of the novel describes the events after Michael's flight from the camp. He is befriended by a man and two women who offer him food, drink and sex. Eventually Michael returns to his mother's room. He is dying. In his delirium he thinks of nothing but returning to the farm to start his garden all over again. The earth has to be tended and nourished, no matter what, even if a teaspoon is the only available tool.[3]

With this final scene the novel has come full circle. Michael has returned to the novel's starting point: his mother's room in Sea Point. In addition, a link is suggested between his last thought of watering the earth with a teaspoon and Michael as a baby, who, because of his harelip, had to be fed with a teaspoon as well.[4] The closing of the circle suggests the futility of Michael's self-imposed task. He has achieved nothing whatsoever and is dying from starvation, but is still clinging to his pipedream of making the earth fertile. This single-minded determination, against all odds, convinces the reader of the importance of Michael's stand and the urgency of his task. The agony of his final days gives him the aura of a hero who, with unflinching integrity, is prepared to make the ultimate sacrifice in order to remain true to that in which he so fervently believes.

This ideal is to tend the earth, to make it fruitful. Michael sees himself exclusively as a gardener: "the truth, the truth about me. I am a gardener".[5] He is of the opinion that if no-one tends the earth, it will become barren so that no life will be possible any more. Although Michael only has an intuitive grasp of this idea, his whole life is an embodiment of it. He himself is too much of a simpleton, a marginal being set apart from the others by his harelip, to be fully aware of the wider implications of his acts. He possesses the inner conviction, however, that what he is doing is absolutely right and the only possible thing for him to do. It is the camp doctor who tries to find an explanation and who gives voice to what he thinks Michael stands for; hence the importance of the second part of the novel.[6] In contrast, Michael himself repeatedly stresses that he has nothing to say, that there is no story to tell. He can be described as a non-personality living through a non-event.

Michael is completely cut off from normal, everyday life. He characterizes himself as a sleepwalker with no needs, "wanting nothing, looking forward to nothing".[7] The level of his awareness approaches that of an animal, with which he is often identified. He hardly notices what goes on around him and is only to a minimal degree conscious of his surroundings: "There seemed nothing to do but live".[8] His life has turned into mere existence. Michael's only desire is to be left alone, to find a piece of land that has not yet been fenced, where he can quietly cultivate the earth and thus be perfectly happy.

Clearly, Michael's wishes are extremely basic, his level of reflection almost non-existent, except for the last few pages of the novel when his thoughts are directly rendered. Because of his adoption of a lifestyle that is totally alien to normal society, Michael can barely be called a victim, even on the occasions when that society intrudes into his life. Michael undergoes the beatings by the soldiers or the internments of the camps without offering any resistance. He seems oblivious to it all, untouched, unabsorbed:

> But when the state stamped Michael with a number and
> gobbled him down it was wasting its time. For Michael
> has passed through the bowels of the state undigested; he
> has emerged from its camps as intact as he emerged
> from its schools and orphanages.[9]

Michael's values are so different from those of society that it has no hold on him any more. He is the quintessential dropout.

Michael K is very much his own man and because of his total
disregard for society and all it represents, he turns into its
opposite, although he himself does not realise this. The novel
depicts a pitiable character who, despite the problems he
encounters, is stubbornly in search of fulfilment. Throughout,
attention is focussed decisively on Michael's ideal and his
determination to realize it; his personality and state of mind
during his ordeal are of secondary importance. As a result,
Michael's life is presented as a meaningful experience, it is a
fascinating case-study. This is made very plain by the doctor:
"Your stay in the camp was merely an allegory - speaking at the
highest level - of how scandalously, how outrageously a meaning
can take up residence in a system without becoming a term in
it".[10]

The allegorical meaning of Michael's life - and of the novel as
a whole - is linked to the process of gradual degradation he
undergoes. Towards the end Michael is almost naked, he only
wears an overall. He feels liquid.[11] He has become almost
disembodied, a spiritual presence, a spirit. It is not difficult for
him to escape from the camp, twice: he is "a great escape
artist",[12] and starvation has made him into a very thin man. This
is the result of the problems he encountered while cultivating the
land. His garden does not produce enough food to sustain him
because he has to contend with all sorts of difficulties that threaten
his life as a gardener: the goats, the deserter, the army, the
guerrillas and their donkeys. Moreover, Michael adamantly
refuses to eat camp food. His rejection of almost all food that does
not come manifestly from the earth is not based on a conscious
decision, but seems mysteriously connected with his tending the
soil and enjoying "the bounty of the earth".[13] Certainly, but
without precisely knowing why, he fervently believes that this
objective is of the utmost importance. That also explains why he
cannot join the guerrillas when he encounters them on the farm:

> ... because enough men had gone off to war saying the
> time for gardening was when the war was over, whereas
> there must be men to stay behind and keep gardening
> alive, or at least the idea of gardening; because once that
> cord was broken, the earth would grow hard and forget
> her children. That was why.[14]

Michael's life is exclusively dedicated to the realization of his
ideal. In order to reach his goal he has to withdraw from society
and become a hermit. His resolve is embedded in the firm belief
that the reason for whatever his intuition dictates him to do will

become clear later on. He is guided by the conviction that life is, must be, a meaningful experience. It is because of his missionary zeal and his freedom that the camp doctor envies him. He would like to join Michael in his search for his utopian garden:

> The garden for which you are presently heading is nowhere and everywhere except in the camps. It is another name for the place where you belong, Michaels, where you do not feel homeless. It is off every map, no road leads to it that is merely a road, and only you know the way.[15]

What the garden represents is not as such spelled out in the novel, but gradually becomes clear through suggestion. When Michael eats his own fruits for the first time, he experiences a sexual ecstasy. He also thanks the earth using the words spoken when receiving Communion. The ripe fruit is evidently the ultimate gift the earth can provide. Through its creative power it produces a life-giving food and through the cultivation of the earth man can foster this creative process. To be aware of this means the acquisition of a fundamental freedom that cannot be obtained in any other way, but it also implies a rejection of almost everything man stands for and the acceptance of man's mortality. This explains why Michael cannot eat camp food any more and why he does not want to leave any traces: he has no children, nor does he want to build a solid house as the Visagies did. He wants to go through life unnoticed, and after his death become one with the earth just like his mother. He has cut all ties with society. His outcast status, his harelip, his reticence and inability to communicate are outward signs of this rift. Instead he has become a tender of the earth: cultivating and eating its fruits, living at the lowest of levels. He is a non-entity as the letter K in his name suggests, and he likes it that way.

The identification of the earth with the creative process is reinforced by frequent references to female symbols. The most important passage in this respect is the one in which Michael is described burying his mother's ashes in the soil of the farm,[16] for it is while performing this ritual, that Michael gets the idea of starting a garden. The shelter he builds is between two rocks in the shape of breasts; the earth is explicitly described as a mother nurturing her fruits as children and frequently reveals the characteristics of a human being.

Michael's attempts to isolate himself from society and to devote his life to the cultivation of his primitive garden are only partially successful. Life outside the farm continually infringes upon it. Michael lives in permanent fear of being discovered. He must hide in a shelter between the rocks; he sleeps during the day and tends his garden only during the night, another female symbol. He must cover up his pumpkins and melons so that they are not detectable. Despite all these precautions the civil war and the camps always catch up with him. Both are metaphors for the never-ending struggle to dominate others, to subjugate the earth and, more generally, to leave some mark, in a vain, human attempt to transcend mortality. The doctor suggests that such a struggle is inherent to man, but futile, as it merely leads to a vicious circle of camps being replaced by other camps. In simple terms, it is impossible to increase universal happiness by waging war. And yet this behavioural pattern is nonetheless the accepted norm and brings with it the fencing in of people as well as land. It is associated, too, by Michael with "huis Morenius", the orphanage where he spent most of his youth.[17] The parallel is clear: the urge to dominate makes man into an orphan in that it separates him from the creative process of the earth. Michael, in contrast, is characterized as a universal soul, who lives outside time and history. The values and norms of society do not apply to him.

The opposition between creative and destructive forces, respectively represented by Michael and the civil war, is also alluded to in the title of the book: *Life and Times of Michael K.* Unlike the novelistic tradition this title refers to, the plot of Coetzee's book is not based on the interaction between the hero and his environment but works in a contrastive way. Michael even refuses to eat the food society offers him in an unequivocal indication of the gap between the two worlds. Only with the humblest and poorest can Michael find some common ground. They pity him and are prepared to extend a helping hand. They are even willing to share their food with him. They are as helpless as he is: pawns in a power struggle they do not understand.

This contrast enhances the allegorical structure of the novel. The particular circumstances are not relevant, the main character remains to a large degree anonymous. Instead two basic responses to life are contrasted. The apparently predominant one is the struggle to constrain and suppress, the other is the need to facilitate the creative energy of the earth. If that is forgotten, the human race is doomed. Superficially, Michael's story seems to revive the myth of the noble primitive living in close contact with nature and rejecting civilization as decadent. Of course Coetzee tackles this theme from quite a different angle. The primitive life Michael leads does not bring him too much happiness. He becomes emaciated and in the end is dying from starvation. The fact that Michael is not left in peace, that he is unable to realize his goal, is the gravest indictment of the society he has left:

> What a pity that to live in times like these a man must be ready to live like a beast. A man who wants to live cannot live in a house with lights in the windows. He must live in a hole and hide by day. A man must live so that he leaves no trace of his living. That is what it has come to.[18]

The destructive forces have overcome the creative ones, hence the very pessimistic undertone of the novel.

Although the novel is situated in the South African context, no mention is made of the skin colour of the different characters, and the novel makes no direct reference to the racial conflict in South Africa. Indirectly, however, racial discrimination is easily recognizable as one of the more repugnant ways of exercising domination over others. But the allegorical treatment of the central theme contributes to giving it a more universal applicability. Michael K, in his suffering and his willingness to sacrifice his life to keep his ideal alive, is a Christ-like figure. In his utter devotion to his self-set task, he is not of this world. Despite his preordained death, he conveys a crucial message about our task as human beings. It is not surprising, therefore, that he is given the name of the archangel Michael or wears the clothes of the St. John's ambulance men. He even manages to gain a disciple: the camp doctor who wants to follow him in his search for his mythical garden. Michael has at least made one person aware of a possible alternative to domination and war, though it is rather doubtful that the doctor will follow his example. This, together with the reaffirmation of the integrity of the individual and a belief in what he can achieve if he puts his mind to it, are the only rays of hope in an otherwise very bleak novel.

Luc Renders

NOTES

[1] J.M. Coetzee, *Life and Times of Michael K*, Johannesburg: Ravan Press, 1983, pp. 155-6.

[2] Ibid., p. 10.

[3] Ibid., p. 250.

[4] Ibid., p. 3.

[5] Ibid., pp. 247-8.

[6] The change of point-of-view in the second part is seen by a number of critics as a shortcoming in the novel.   They consider the doctor's explanation to be superfluous because the novel's meaning is fully understandable without it.   I do not share their opinion.   I believe the second part gives greater relevance to Michael's story as it makes him into a victim of the war and consequently gives the war a reality it does not have in Michael's life.   Moreover, as the doctor sympathizes with Michael, he reinforces the validity of the ideal Michael is striving for.

[7] *Life and Times of Michael K*, p. 94.

[8] Ibid., p. 91.

[9] Ibid., p. 221.

[10] Ibid., p. 228.

[11] Ibid., p. 237.

[12] Ibid., p. 228.

[13] Ibid., p. 162.

[14] Ibid., p. 150.

[15] Ibid., p. 228.

[16] Ibid., pp. 80-81.

[17] Ibid., p. 143.

[18] Ibid., p. 135.

10.

TOURNIER, BORBORYGMUS AND BORBOROLOGY: REVERBERATIONS OF EATING EACH OTHER

In considering the resonance of Tournier's intextinal rumblings, it is not inappropriate to begin by invoking an infamous and enigmatic spectre of those stark and chilling Far Northern wastes to which the author himself returns, briefly but significantly, in several of his writings:

> The Wendigo,
> The Wendigo!
> Its eyes are ice and indigo!
> Its blood is rank and yellowish!
> Its voice is hoarse and bellowish!
> Its tentacles are slithery,
> And scummy,
> Slimy,
> Leathery!
> Its lips are hungry blubbery,
> And smacky,
> Sucky,
> Rubbery!
>
> The Wendigo!
> The Wendigo!
> I saw it just a friend ago
> Last night it lurked in Canada;
> Tonight, on your veranda!
> As you are lolling hammockwise
> It contemplates you stomachwise
> You loll,
> It contemplates,
> It lollops,
> The rest is merely gulps and gollops.[1]

The Windigo, of course, is that solitary creature fashioned centuries ago by the imagination - or perhaps the experience - of the Canadian Algonquin Indian tribes. Terrible in aspect, but recognizably human, it is feared most because of its insatiable craving for human flesh. As such it is perhaps the most awful phantom of the desperate, wracking hunger which may accompany and threaten survival amid the isolation of that extreme Northern example of the human landscape. Indeed, the term "Windigo psychosis" is employed today by the psychiatric profession to characterize a mental disorder reported not infrequently in the area in question. The outstanding symptom, predictably enough, is an intense, compulsive, desire to eat one's fellows ...

However, although characterized there as in all today's cultures as an aberration, a severe case of psycho-social dysfunctioning, the urge to cannibalism, it may be conjectured, and related experiences could rather represent, at least in several contemporary novels, our yearning for some resolution of solitude, some visceral contact, some symbiosis to heal the fracture, the fissure astride which we exist. In which case, of course, traces of the "Windigo psychosis" may be just as much present amongst academic groves and suburban gardens, as amongst the tepees of the Ojibwa, the Micmac, the Cree and the Blackfoot of Northern and Eastern Canada ...

In literature, until recent times, and Shakespeare here would be a good example, cannibalism was indeed "dysfunctional", the image - however fascinating - of deep evil and chaos, of a world turned upside down. Indeed, so unthinkable was the whole business that it was suitable meat for outrageous satire, as in Swift's 1728 *Modest Proposal* to resolve the infant Irish problem:

> I have been assured by a very knowing American of my acquaintance in London, that a young healthy child, well nurs'd, is, at a year old, a most delicious, nourishing and wholesome food, whether stewed, roasted, baked or boiled; and I make no doubt that it will equally serve in a *fricassée* or a *ragoût*.[2]

And yet, paradoxically, in spiritual belief - and across diverse cultures - any heinous aspect has often been put aside. Many primitive societies accepted as unproblematical the independent potency of flesh and blood, their status therefore as transferable assets which could, even should, be absorbed back into the tribe in order to preserve or enhance certain characteristics. Nor can one ignore the uneasy significance of the year 1215 A.D., when Pope Innocent III convoked the Fourth Lateran Council - virtually the entire Catholic world - in order to endorse the *reality* of the Eucharist as an act of pure, sacred, cannibalism ... the host and wine being promoted by the doctrine of trans-substantiation beyond the symbolic to the actual.

Somewhat in line with this latter tradition, in the literature of the last twenty years or so, I take as an initial indication of a provocatively sympathetic re-consideration of cannibalism the reflective and renewed appropriation of the Crusoe myth, with its characteristic investigation of solitude and man's ability to deal with it; one could cite writers, for example, such as Muriel Spark, J.M. Coetzee, Jane Gardam, Alain Hervé and, of course, Michel Tournier. For each of them, cannibalism, relatively marginal in Defoe's original novel, has become, both in real and figurative terms, much more insistent ...

Moreover, in the case of Tournier, his first novel, *Vendredi ou les limbes du Pacifique*, also announces the basic ingredients that will be retained in the novels to follow. The choice of Crusoe as first hero, first victim and first initiate poses the question of human relationships, or lack of them, from the outset: Crusoe without Friday or Crusoe with Friday; island isolation or island community; inward anguish or outward appropriation; devouring ourselves or devouring each other? But, whereas Defoe's hero had painstakingly and retrospectively reconstituted the society he had lost, Tournier's Crusoe, under the prospective tutelage of Friday and amid a disturbing semiology of vultures, octopuses and vampires, replaces the intellectual and moral with the sensual, discovering an inventive approach to life which gives rise to a new ethic, a new art, a new eroticism and a new communion. Defoe's Friday escapes the cannibals only to be cannibalized "imperialistically" by Crusoe; Tournier's Friday escapes the cannibals only to cannibalize "evangelically" Crusoe! - or perhaps also to be cannibalized once more, but differently.

Although the primary interest here lies in briefly monitoring the *existential* reverberations of such writing, there are undoubtedly other echoes audible within this first work which recur, and would bear further analysis in another setting. One to which Tournier seems to make particular reference, for example, - in his dedication of the novel to the North African immigrant labourers in France - is geo-political in nature: the exchange between Crusoe and Friday transposing that between Europe and the Third World, with Western man in the guise of Crusoe· as, first, exploiter and ingester, and, thereafter, beneficiary and transfusee!

Another echo that continues and grows in the subsequent writings is the association of cannibalism with sexuality: Crusoe in the "souille" eating the sundry productions of his own body, and Friday expressing into a baby vulture's mouth the rotting animal flesh he has masticated himself into "une manière de lait épais"[3] are sufficient to begin to recall the *analogie très profonde* to which Claude Lévi-Strauss had once pointed, and which is implicit in the French "consommer", applicable - alas! - to both sex and steak ... Anglophones, happily, prefer to differentiate.

In his *Petites proses* Tournier invokes, as symptomatic in this regard, the praying mantis:

> ... le cerveau du mâle exerce une action inhibitrice sur l'éjaculation du sperme. Si elle veut être fécondée, la femelle n'a donc pour ressource que de broyer entre ses dents la boîte crânienne du malheureux inhibé qui éjacule alors en toute liberté.[4]

A somewhat trenchant response to frustration or hunger, one might think, but nevertheless procreative cannibalism of the most admirably intransigeant and resolute kind.

To move on, there can be no doubt about the importance of food in Tournier's world: he revels in the regular Hôtel Drouant lunches with his etymological "copains" of the Académie Goncourt; he even receives vagrant professors with delectable panache. But, most of all, there is the massive, manic, eating to be encountered in the novels. Take, for instance, this delicious "image d'Epinal" from *Le Roi des aulnes*:

> Göring vêtu d'un coquet kimono bleu pâle était attablé devant un demi-sanglier dont il brandissait une cuisse, comme la massue d'Hercule. Le lion assis à ses côtés suivait passionnément l'évolution de la pièce de vénerie au-dessus de sa tête, et donnait des coups de gueule lents et sans conviction dans sa direction quand elle se rapprochait. Finalement le grand veneur y mordit à pleines dents, et pendant quelques instants sa figure disparut derrière le monstrueux gigot. Puis, la bouche pleine, il le tendit au lion qui y planta ses crocs à son tour. Et ce fut un va-et-vient régulier de la pièce de vénerie entre les deux ogres qui se regardaient affectueusement en mastiquant des paquets de chair noire et musquée.[5]

Or else Herod's delightful *amuse-gueules* tendered to the three
Kings, Gaspard, Melchior and Balthazar:

> Il y avait des foies de carrelets mêlés à de la laitance de
> lamproies, des cervelles de paons et de faisans, des yeux
> de mouflons et des langues de chamelons, des ibis farcis
> au gingembre, et surtout un vaste ragoût dont la sauce
> brune encore mijotante noyait des vulves de jument et
> des génitoires de taureaux.[6]

Both Göring and Herod are, of course, examples - incarnations
(sic! so to speak) - of the ogre, who appears in his most developed
form in the character, Abel Tiffauges. Through such a character
Tournier is able to continue to explore still further, not only that
patent obsession with the orifice, in all its functions, already
manifest in the first novel, but also the question of predation, in
which the contiguity of "servir/asservir", "porter/emporter",
"aimer/dévorer" projects a far more enigmatic personage than
traditional popular opinion would have.

Tiffauges, from the outset then, is an ogre/cannibal in
gestation. Attracted instinctively to raw meat, he is soon initiated
by Nestor into the further pleasures of the alimentary process,
graduating ere long to the vampiric ecstasy of cleaning a bigger
boy's bleeding knee with his own trembling tongue and lips. But
certainly not all his proclivities are as idiosyncratic ... for
photographic appropriation is soon discovered as at least equally, if
temporarily, satiating. Tiffauges's special joy, whilst a young
garage-owner at the conveniently-named Porte des Ternes in
Paris, is to drive through the streets, his camera nestling snugly
between his thighs, his eyes alert for likely prey: "Je me plais
ainsi équipé d'un sexe énorme, gainé de cuir, dont l'oeil de cyclope
s'ouvre comme l'éclair quand je lui dis 'Regarde!' et se referme
inexorablement sur ce qu'il a vu.".[7] The allusion to a sort of
Cyclopean phallus reveals unequivocally the lineage that is being
invoked. For Tiffauges informs a tradition, recalled referentially
and reverently throughout the novel, which embraces not only
Cyclops, but Cronos, Tiresias, Orion, the Erl-King, Colin-Maillard,
Bluebeard and Gilles de Rais. Thus, significantly, the common,
even banal, photographic experience - as elsewhere in Tournier,
in, for example, *La Goutte d'or*, "Les Suaires de Véronique" - is
portrayed as intrinsically cannibalistic: the incorporation of a
"persona" through an ever-available aperture. Not dissimilar,
perhaps, are the other, primarily "phoric" experiences - the
carrier-pigeons, the hunting at Rominten, the recruiting at
Kaltenborn. Certainly, Tiffauges himself is under few illusions,

as, deciphering progressively the various signs he is absorbing, he moves forward - lovingly and hungrily - towards that final identification with the Erl-King which will be his own particular apotheosis. Thus, his steamy shower-room fantasizing in the para-military school which he ultimately serves is entirely lucid: "Tous ces enfants bouillent dans un chaudron géant avant d'être mangés ...".[8] A comparably festive aura emanates towards the end of *Gilles et Jeanne* from Gilles's castle - inevitably called with historical veracity "Tiffauges" - as the smoke and smell of young, carbonized, flesh wend their semiotic way heavenwards ... Gilles, too, is approaching his final reintegration with an, the, Other - this time with Jeanne d'Arc.

The key, perhaps, to an understanding of the significance of cannibalism and its various derivatives in Tournier, and indeed in much recent literature, comes in *Les Météores*. There, it is suggested that originally, prior to birth, every individual was part of a couple, that the division person/society, self/other, can only be understood as an agonisingly degraded version of that "zénith de la perfection humaine", the identical twins. Thus we are all "sans-pareils" in search of plenitude. It is Paul, estranged now from his twin Jean, but seeking to re-discover that original cellular unity, Jean-Paul, who articulates the notion most clearly:

> Ecoute cette merveille, et mesure ses immenses implications: tout homme a primitivement un frère jumeau. Toute femme enceinte porte *deux* enfants dans son sein. Mais le plus fort ne tolère pas la présence d'un frère avec lequel il faut tout partager. Il l'étrangle dans le ventre de sa mère, et l'ayant étranglé, il le mange, puis il vient seul au monde, souillé par ce crime originel, condamné à la solitude et trahi par le stigmate de sa taille monstrueuse. L'humanité est composée d'ogres, des hommes forts, oui avec des mains d'étrangleurs et des dents de cannibale.[9]

- which would seem to justify the picture of the curious, egg-enclosed twins in complementary foetal position on the cover of the Folio edition of the novel, fraught with its very graphic evocation of sexuality and cannibalism. But what is perhaps most important to retain from the above passage is not so much the cannibalism proposed as original sin, but man's *continuing* cannibalistic potential, because of that lost paradise of perfect companionship for which we yearn ... voraciously! Although cannibalism is a subject that has always elicited a vaguely prurient, if fearful, fascination - hence the journalistic mileage accorded to the

Andean air-disaster of the 1970s - of late the recurrent value to be attached to its appearance in literature would seem to have become far more exemplary ... cannibalism as an antidote - of physicality, proximity, passion and contact - to that isolation which now defines the human condition.

In conclusion - and validating joyfully once more the merit of the general theme of literary gastronomy, while confounding, I believe, the petty burps of its assailants - one can reasonably begin by re-iterating, for Tournier and others, the importance of the digestive tract as a resounding point of reference: ingestion, digestion, defecation. The assimilation of what is beneficial and the elimination of bacteria-bearing waste-products carry with them the corollary of improved health, greater energy, and resistance to malaise or disease. An ailing Crusoe is thus nourished by Friday, a truncated Tiffauges feeds, still more patently, on children, that most privileged and wondrous of species in Tournier's scheme of things.

In psychological terms, Tournier's preoccupations are not far removed from the notions of "projective identification" and "incorporation" proposed earlier this century by Freud and, more provocatively, by Melanie Klein - for whom the act of taking milk from one's mother's breast was never as uncomplicated as I used to believe it was ... Certainly Tournier seems overtly Kleinian in the Indian experience he recounts in *Des clefs et des serrures*:

> Et il y a la faim, et il y a les enfants. Ce que j'ai vu en Inde de plus beau, exaltant, émouvant à pleurer, enthousiasmant à crier (...) C'était un vieux camion-citerne. Des groupes d'enfants haillonneux se groupaient sagement derrière la citerne. Le chauffeur descendu actionnait un gros robinet qui lâchait une bouillie de riz dans le petit bol que tendait un enfant.[10]

Indeed, having admitted how much he coveted the role of driver of this marvellous vehicle, Tournier goes on to reveal how, later, in a dream, he formulated an even more profound desire: "... j'ai rêvé d'une métamorphose plus exaltante encore: être le camion-citerne lui-même et, telle une énorme truie aux cent tétines généreuses, donner mon ventre en pâture aux petits Indiens affamés.".[11] This apparent inversion by which the ogre devours, but is *also* devoured, would seem to promote as the *ultimate* - a new Grail, an absolute need - a sort of cannibalism, but reciprocal, an *inter*action, a veritable exchange, that verges on symbiosis itself. It recalls that so-called primitive ritual in which the cannibalistic act honoured, even deified, one's victim as well as strengthening one's self. An integration and a mutual perpetuation ... Several of Tournier's relationships could reasonably be perceived in this way: Friday and Crusoe (and subsequently the cabin-boy), Idriss and Europe, Véronique and Hector, Tiffauges and the children, Gilles and Jeanne.

Nor, of course, are such situations and preoccupations in any way confined to Tournier. Ogre/child may in some cases become kidnapper/ kidnapped, torturer/tortured, lover/loved, prosecutor/prosecuted, terrorist/ hostage, coloniser/colonised etc. ... but certainly John Fowles, J.M. Coetzee, Wittig, Genêt, Mailer, Malraux, Golding, Ted Hughes, Muriel Spark, Camus, Duras, Hartley, Mishima, Doris Lessing, Lu Hsün and others too would bear close examination in a comparative study that remains to be done. For all explore very similar metonymical avatars of humanity's all-devouring desire to touch, embrace and fuse in a violent, voluptuous, and almost apoplectic reaction to the unacceptable pain of twentieth century solitude.

In that way eating one other would seem to have become a consummation devoutly to be wished!

David Bevan

NOTES

[1] This poem by Ogden Nash is taken from *Windigo* (ed. J.R. Colombo), Saskatoon: Western Producer Prairie Books, 1982, p. 127.

[2] J. Swift, *Satires and Personal Writings*, London: Oxford University Press, 1962, p. 23.

[3] M. Tournier, *Vendredi ou les limbes du Pacifique*, Paris: Gallimard, 1972, p. 173; "a sort of thick milk". In each case the translations are my own.

[4] M. Tournier, *Petites proses*, Paris: Gallimard, 1986, p. 119; "... the head of the male has an inhibiting effect on the ejaculation of the sperm. If she wishes to be fertilized, the female's only recourse is to crush between her teeth the cranium of the inhibited wretch who then ejaculates with total freedom."

[5] M. Tournier, *Le Roi des aulnes*, Paris: Gallimard, 1977, p. 322; "Göring, dressed in a smart, pale-blue kimono, was seated at table in front of a side of